Hell in the
Hallway,
Light

at the
Door

Also by Ellen Debenport . . .

The Five Principles: A Guide to Practical Spirituality

Hell in the Hallway, Light at the Door

When one door closes, another one opens, but it can be hell in the hallway.

How to Move Gracefully Through Change into Renewed and Abundant Life

Ellen Debenport

BALBOA
PRESS

A DIVISION OF HAY HOUSE

Balboa Press books may be ordered through booksellers or by contacting:

Balboa Press
A Division of Hay House
1663 Liberty Drive
Bloomington, IN 47403
www.balboapress.com
1 (877) 407-4847

Print information available on the last page.

ISBN: 978-1-5043-4058-8 (sc)
ISBN: 978-1-5043-4059-5 (e)

Library of Congress Control Number: 2015914949

Balboa Press rev. date: 10/22/2015

Contents

Part 3 - Opening the Door

Introduction

I wish I knew who originally said, *When one door closes, another one opens, but it can be hell in the hallway.* I heard it from my mother, who was quoting a speaker she heard at a conference.

At first, it's amusing. The image of being in a hallway, looking for a doorway out, usually elicits a chuckle of recognition.

Then memories of hell may surface for anyone who has been through a difficult change. We've all been there.

The first time I spoke about the hallway, the audience's response astounded me. People couldn't wait to tell me their personal stories. Everyone seemed to be in a time of transition or knew someone who was. At last, they had a name and a visual image for what they were going through. They were in the hallway!

Simply knowing what to call it and how to think about this period of uncertainty in your life can be healing.

A door has closed, but another will open.

The sun will rise on a new day.

Your experience had a beginning and will have an end, if not in physical form then at least in your mind and heart, as you make peace with reality. The hallway represents change, and you've survived change before.

The hallway is not simply to be endured. It can be a place of recovery and reflection, of growth and understanding, of human love and deeper connection with Spirit.

I hope this book will help you stay conscious and awake to the gifts life has brought you, even if you have no idea what the future holds.

A COMMON THREAD

Any discussion of the hallway falls naturally into three parts—what puts you in the hallway, what you do while you're there, and how you manage to leave it. Whether the door that closed for you involved death, divorce, job loss, illness or a major alteration in your family or life circumstances, you are in a hallway, and all hallways have elements in common.

Some might argue that grieving a death is different from, say, bankruptcy. Or ending a relationship is different from losing a job.

The details are certainly different. But I maintain the *spiritual* challenge is the same whenever you go through a major change. The work of the hallway is to accept what has happened, unwrap the gifts that have been delivered in this strange and unexpected package, and design the next phase of your life.

Nearly everyone who has been through a difficult transition recounts a divine element, and this book freely discusses God, prayer and spirituality. I find very few people take offense at such language, but you are welcome to tweak the ideas presented here to fit your personal beliefs.

No matter the language used to describe them, our needs in the hallway are similar in any circumstances. You will probably need:

* To accept strength, comfort and guidance from other people.
* To spend time alone, to be quiet, take walks, journal, create or pray.
* To forgive people, groups or circumstances.
* To become willing to see the gifts in the situation.
* To understand and accept a new reality.
* And eventually, to open a door to the next chapter of your life.

I consider these elements to be spiritual. And by that I mean *of the Spirit* that each of us embodies, as we are fully human and fully divine.

This is not about religion. The journey through the hallway is within you.

THOSE WHO HAVE GONE BEFORE YOU

I wish I could offer you *10 Quick Steps Through the Hallway! Feel better today! Solve all your problems with one short book!* But that would diminish your experience.

In this book, you will read the stories of real people who have been through the hallway and survived, even maximized their time in the darkness. I am struck by the raw honesty of their sharing, the sometimes searing pain they describe and the redemption they found when they opened a new door.

One friend who read an early draft complained the stories were depressing. Seriously? I find them magnificently uplifting! Every one of them is about overcoming adversity through the power of God and the human spirit. I hope reading about the experiences of others who have navigated their way through the hallway into renewed life will be as instructive and inspiring as anything I could tell you.

You will hear these people describe how they survived some of the most difficult episodes of their lives. Parts Two and Three of this book will break out the elements of their spiritual work so you may look more closely at their process. Then you will see how they took responsibility for designing the lives they wanted as they emerged into a new day.

If they can do it, so can you.

Some of the people whose stories you will read were interviewed by me in person, and others sent emails when I requested hallway stories. Each person is quoted directly—no composites, no fictionalizing—and only a few first names have been changed. Wherever you see a full name, it is real, and of course all the stories are used with permission.

These stories are not out of the ordinary, except for the people who were involved. No one made headlines or history. But that's the point. Change is part of life, and how you manage each new phase of your life—especially when you did not seek it—is one of the primary ways your soul grows through this human experience.

I am honored and grateful these stories were shared

with me. But those quoted here offered their experiences in the hope of helping *you*.

You will surely identify with some of them. Their circumstances fall primarily into the Big Three categories of life: health, relationships and money. You might not see the exact details of your story in this book, but remember the spiritual work is the same in any hallway. The circumstances that brought it about are secondary.

I would caution you not to compare pain, not to label yours as greater or less than someone else's. It's unlikely your pain is worse than any other human being has ever suffered, although it might feel that way right now. But also don't minimize what you feel, just because the change in your life appears less dramatic than some.

Your life is offering gifts designed especially for you. Notice and accept them. Take all the good you can from your personal hallway before you open the next door and step, blinking, into the light.

A Word About Hell

As much as I love spiritual seekers and surround myself with them, talking to them is sometimes difficult. Especially when I suggest certain events in our lives are just plain awful.

When I talk about hell in the hallway, they challenge me:

Does it have to be hell? What do you mean by "hell" anyway?

That's judgmental. Don't label it as bad. It is what it is.

If we affirm it's going to be hell, then won't it be?

Don't we create our own hell?

Yes, we do, that's the point. The goal of this book is to create something better.

But I'm not going to pretend that every experience in life is happy, joyful or beneficial. Not all feelings are equally desirable. Some events in our lives hurt like hell and irrevocably change the landscape of our world.

This book is designed to guide you through those times.

If you can take change in stride, leap hurdles in a single bound and stay spiritually centered no matter what happens in your life, you don't need this book.

If you want to explore the hallway without using the

word "hell," fine by me. If you choose not to designate *any* circumstance as undesirable, if you believe all emotions and all events are created equal, I get your point. In the absolute cosmic scheme of things, our lives are unfolding perfectly.

But we are here for the human experience, and it often feels messy and complicated.

So if you are going through change and transition and have days when you don't want to get out of bed . . .

Or days you can't stop crying . . .

Or days when you think if you start to cry, you'll never stop . . .

On those days when you walk around with a hole in your chest that feels as if a cold wind is whistling through your body . . .

And you can't imagine ever feeling good again . . .

I call those days hell. And this book is for you.

Part One

Welcome to the Hallway

This place where you are right now
God circled on a map for you.

—*Hafiz (tr. Daniel Ladinsky)*

1 The Hallway

When one door closes, another one opens, but it can be hell in the hallway.

The hallway is that place between jobs, between relationships, during a major illness or after a permanent change or crisis. Life as you know it has ended, and you're not sure what's coming next.

Groping through the darkness, you might trip and fall down, or give up and cry. Or cuss. You can't even begin to see a doorway out.

Yet this time of transition can be made meaningful and useful. It could become the launching pad for the rest of your life.

That's what this book is about—how to make use of your time in the hallway, then walk out into the light, whether it's the brilliant light of a new perspective or the dawning light of gradual acceptance.

Everyone spends time in the hallway. Chances are good you are in one now or know someone who is. Some typical hallways:

* Someone you love has died.
* A child is leaving home
* A baby is on the way

* A medical test is pending, a scary diagnosis has turned life upside-down, or recovery from illness is uncertain or impossible
* A new marriage is under way, or divorce is fresh
* You are going through unemployment, bankruptcy or foreclosure.
* You are being forced to move, or you are choosing to move.
* You are changing jobs or retiring.

Of course, not every difficult situation counts as a major life transition. A fight with your spouse, living with an obstinate 2-year-old or suffering a bout of flu are typical episodes that thankfully will come to an end. The hallway in contrast is marked by a definite door closing, an unmistakable shift in circumstances. It's a change that initially might beat you down but inevitably calls you higher.

This experience is an opportunity for nothing less than spiritual transformation. It might seem to have been forced upon you, and your first task might be to recover from heartbreak, betrayal, fear, grief or anger. But this painful period can be redeemed and, with conscious and deliberate attention, you will emerge with a changed view of yourself and new possibilities for your life.

When the dark night comes upon you— not *if* it will, but *when* it does—it's part of your soul's curriculum. Something will happen that you didn't want to have happen. The first thing you do is everything you *can* do to try to make it go away. When you discover your personal power is not big enough to make it go away, if you surrender to it . . . a strange feeling will come over you that you don't want it to end too soon, because you really do want everything it came to give you.

Mary Morrissey

HOW DID I GET HERE?

Doors close in different ways. Some slam shut: You get fired, your spouse walks out, your body breaks down, a loved one dies. Sometimes disability or illness in the immediate family rearranges all your plans.

Other doors slowly creak shut: You plan for retirement for years, or you prepare for the last child to leave home. Transition starts long before the event. Even though you know it's coming, the closing door means a permanent shift in your life.

Sometimes you close the door yourself and—boldly or with trepidation—step into the hallway: You end a relationship, move to a new city, start a new career, or leave a job without having the next one lined up.

And some hallways are invisible to the observer; they are only experienced within. This is often part of a spiritual shift, when divine discontent prompts you to close doors and undertake complete transformation, like a caterpillar entering a cocoon. You may or may not be aware that, at some level, you volunteered for it.

We will discuss each type of change in more detail. Just remember, all hallways begin with something that has ended, and the experience might look and feel like profound loss at first, might seem as if your life has gone terribly awry. But change is the only way life can be made better, and "better" often requires leaving behind what was merely good.

Hallways sometimes look worse than they are. We might dread them and resist them, resent them and avoid them with far more energy than it would take to move through them.

Terry Anderson, a reporter who was held hostage in Lebanon for nearly seven years, said: "It would be a shame if I went through that experience and didn't change. I had lots of time to think about who I am, what I believe, what's really important to me."

Or fighter pilot Charlie Plumb, who was shot down and held as a prisoner of war in Vietnam for six years. He first considered it a colossal waste of time. Yet years after he was freed, he said it was a "beautiful gift."

A gift! Trapped in an 8 by 8 foot cell, not knowing whether he would live from day to day.

He said nothing could have taught him more.

"There's great value in getting blown out of the sky once in a while," Plumb said in a speech. "There's great value in that wakeup call that forces you and me to re-examine the way we're doing business. Said a little differently, adversity is a horrible thing to waste."

I am astonished at the gifts that can be received in the midst of painful adjustments to a new life. Going through chemo, losing a child, being laid off, saying good-bye too soon. You don't have to claim such events were blessings in disguise. You don't have to believe they were necessary. But good can always come from them.

These days, I've come to respect the hallway. It's not so scary to me now because I know good stuff can happen there. Growth happens there. These days I can willingly walk into the hallway and say, "O.K. bring it on!" and know that when I have done my work, a new door will pop right open, and I will walk through, confident of the new and exciting experiences the Universe is eager to provide.

Rachel

Rachel makes the hallway sound downright happy, doesn't she? But she knows the depths of its pain. You will read her story in Part Two.

Here's another view, from a man who experienced excruciating grief after a friend's death. His full story is in Part Two as well.

It is said that when God closes one door, he opens another. But he had thrown me face first into the pitch-black hallway and slammed shut the door to a normal life... let alone a joyful one. And there was no hope of another door anywhere.

Jerry Magar

AN INSIDE JOB

People regularly tell me, "What doesn't kill you makes you stronger," which is patently untrue. Sometimes what doesn't kill you ruins your life, if you let it. Some people are forever weakened by events and never re-emerge. And sometimes, what kills you is supposed to do exactly that. Death eventually will claim each of us, and the process of dying can be the most profound, healing and loving transition of all.

There is no disgrace in scrambling to find your bearings in the hallway, and you will read more in later chapters about that initial confusion.

An oncologist once told me that high anxiety seems to short-circuit people's brains. He called it "cerebral fibrillation," which I suppose is medical humor to describe what the Buddhists call monkey mind, a brain that can't focus, become still or settle on solutions.

But then bravery kicks in. The doctor said the best and bravest people he sees are ordinary women, mostly middle-aged, who would never think of themselves as courageous. The key, he said, is to become comfortable with not being in control. There's so much we don't know. Even the doctors and experts don't know.

You won't always know how you ended up in a dark and unfamiliar place, or why or how long you'll be there. Regardless of what happened in your life, what happens next is an inside job. And therein lies the key to maneuvering through each hallway to a new door.

You are the creator of your experience, which means you have more power than you have yet imagined. You are not a victim of circumstance or of other people's problems, and this is not a test from God. You are a spiritual being having a human experience, and you have the ability to call forth divine energy, even in the darkest hallway.

Look closely, and you might see a crack of light shining underneath the next door.

BITS OF WISDOM

* The hallway is that place of uncertainty when one door has closed and the next has not yet opened.
* Doors might slam shut or creak shut. Some you close yourself. But all hallways are journeys of inner transformation.
* Change is the only way life gets better. Sometimes receiving what is better means releasing what was good.
* It takes less energy to move through the hallway than to avoid or deny it.
* No matter how a door was closed, the work of the hallway is an inside job.
* Your growth in the hallway, and the next door you open, are within your creative power.

THIS PRAYER IS FOR YOU

Divine love and support are with you as you dwell in this time of uncertainty. You may be feeling loss in your life and dread for the future, or you might be thrilled with anticipation. Either way, your life is changing.

No matter what brought you into the hallway, know you are not alone. So very many have been here before you, and a new door *will* open. You will leave this experience with gifts and insights.

Turn within now. Search more deeply than you might ever have searched before. Inside, you will discover that all the guidance, clarity and strength you need are available to you.

Immerse yourself in the awareness of a Presence that is stronger, more powerful and more loving than you can imagine. You are never separate from this divine Presence; you are one of its many expressions. Draw from it like a deep well to nourish yourself on this journey.

2 Doors That Slam

The most dramatic and difficult hallway experiences often start abruptly. A day dawns routinely and ends with life having changed forever.

A phone call brings news of a death. A job ends. Divorce papers are served. The doctor's diagnosis will mean months or years of treatment. You don't know how long the upheaval will last or what's behind the next door.

Sometimes a door slams so loudly, it reverberates for the rest of your life.

Consider these stories, and witness the resilience, healing and growth of those involved:

SUDDEN HALLWAYS

Russell used to lose his voice every Christmas. For years, during the holidays, Russell couldn't talk. He had no way to explain that on Christmas Day in 1992, his younger brother had committed suicide.

"Over the next days, weeks and years, I was in the hallway in a real way," Russell said.

"I grew up in a very Ozzie and Harriet neighborhood,

and I really thought I came from the perfect family. Holes were blown wide open in the fabric of my life.

"I remember thinking, 'How am I going to explain this to my children?' and I didn't even have kids yet. I remember thinking, 'What kind of a brother would let his brother spiral so far out that there was no coming back?'

"I found myself unable to spend time in grief and healing with my family because I was too busy racing back and forth between past and future. Of course I blamed myself (and I wasn't the only one—there was a small group of us). I had no idea how a family was supposed to be after something like this."

Russell spiraled downward, working longer and harder—sometimes all night— resenting family and friends.

"I hated myself, I hated my family, and most nights I went to sleep wishing I wouldn't wake up. If there were a hell and I had woken up in hell, it probably would not have looked any different."

April had arranged the perfect life for herself. She was a marketing research executive with a doctorate in public policy, and she was teaching statistics and research at a local university—all by the time she was 31 years old.

Then one day, she bent over to place a pen in her briefcase and felt her back go out.

"Within the next few days, I lost sensation in my left leg and my ability to walk without assistance. Back surgery soon followed, along with intensive therapy and several months off work," April wrote.

One doctor insisted she should take addictive narcotics.

One coworker said, "Look at you, disabled for life. And so young! What a shame."

April's boss encouraged her to leave the company in the eighth month of her recovery.

"I decided to step away from the everyday noise and move into a place of mindful, peaceful healing," she said. "I prayed—oh, did I pray—I listened, and I spent less time with the Less Supportive and learned to redefine who I was from the ground up."

Kat adored the grandparents who supported and encouraged her as her guardians. She and her grandfather were devastated when her grandmother died of breast cancer, but as months went by, they began to "laugh a little more and cry a little less," Kat said.

Then one Saturday, 18-year-old Kat discovered her grandfather had collapsed on the floor of the den, dead of a burst aneurysm in his neck.

"Almost the instant he died, I was in the hallway. In the hallway, calling for help. In the hallway, spinning with fear and shock and anguish. In the hallway, thinking this was not real and mostly thinking, 'What about me? What do I do now?'

"I struggled to survive every minute of every day for several weeks. In that hallway, I felt abandoned and isolated and emotionally wrecked. In that hallway, I raged at God. In that hallway, I thought suicide seemed like the easiest way out of that emotional hell."

THE PASSAGE THROUGH

How does anyone survive the hallway? Time. Effort. Grace. Ultimately, it is a spiritual journey.

Before it ends, you might pass through long periods of darkness. Sometimes it seems impossible to release the anger, blame, fear or guilt. You might feel you've lost your connection with the divine, and inner voices of guidance fall silent, drowned out by the cacophony of emotion.

Sometimes life just hurts. We are not on earth to transcend our humanity but to experience it fully. We came into human form because we could learn something here we couldn't learn otherwise.

Kat's grandparents were among six of her family members who died within seven months. Even so, Kat knew there had to be relief for her misery. She relied on the intense support of her teenage friends.

"Finally, after many weeks of turmoil and darkness, I found a door out of that hellish hallway. I found that God was with me all the while and that he never abandoned me, even though I felt like he had. God sent me angels to help me escape. I was reminded as I saw that first, slight glimmer of light, that beyond the hallway of depression, there was a world filled with light and love and joy and possibility."

Kat also gave back, making a point to help others in need. She focused on friends who were experiencing loss, breakups, illnesses including AIDS and challenges with jobs or school.

"Assisting others is an excellent way to get out of the

hallway, if even for only an hour or day or week or two," she said.

Russell, in the years since his brother's suicide, has put together a happy marriage with children and stepchildren.

"When I get some objectivity, this is the hallway that I see: a passageway between what *was* to what *will be*, a conduit from possibility to presence," he said. "If chaos is a place of all-potential, then being willing to move into the hallway without resistance is real faith."

April, who struggled to walk, made a conscious decision to heal. She focused on a mental vision of her perfection or oneness with Source, her divine blueprint of well-being, even while those around her argued.

"My family was convinced that I should spend more time expressing my pain. They worried that this 'trust of my perfection' talk was *not* healthy, that I was not facing the reality of my situation."

But April did heal, never taking her eyes off her inner vision of perfection, seeing only the divine being that is her true nature.

She regained most of the feeling in her leg and finally could walk without a cane. She focused on her teaching, which fed her soul, and spent time resting and taking care of herself.

"To heal, I had to find my own path apart from the perceptions and criticisms of others—to fight for my ability, not my disability—and distance myself from the doubt, anxiety and toxicity of others.

"I had to become centered in the Source, in my perfection that is not defined by my career choices, education or others' comments. My perfection just 'is.'"

BITS OF WISDOM

* Life can change in a day, a phone call, a word or a look. A door slams, and you're in the hallway.
* Abrupt changes might begin a descent into hell, but hang on. The hallway is a passageway, not a final destination.
* Your life may be chaos, but chaos is a place of pure potential. Move into it with faith.
* Sometimes life hurts. We are not on earth to transcend our humanity but to experience it fully.
* As you walk through uncertainty, keep your eye singly focused on your divine perfection.

THIS PRAYER IS FOR YOU

Everything has changed. Everything may be different from now on.

And yet, the Presence never leaves you. It guides, supports and loves you, whether you can feel it today or not.

In this period of uncertainty, know that the prayers of all who have ever been thrust into a dark hallway are with you. Their love reaches back to pull you forward.

Life might never be the same again. But someday, in ways you cannot yet imagine, you will know that all is well.

3 Marilynn's Story:
Finally Feeling Worthy

By Marilynn King

The longest hallway of my lifetime started a week before my 20th birthday. I'd moved hundreds of miles from family and home to attend college in a warm place and had chosen Texas because it sounded wild and exciting.

One Friday night, a gal friend and I drove into Dallas to hit the bars, and it was well past closing time before we flopped down on her bed to pass out.

An intruder with a very large knife woke us up, and a 22-year hallway opened up to swallow me.

The police called it "double aggravated assault," a sanitized description of a brutal, violent act. The rapist was caught and confessed, but that didn't affect my reaction to the two hours that changed my life forever. And besides, the little weasel fled the country rather than face trial.

At 19 years old, I was sassy, self-confident and sure I could do and be anything I wanted. I was enjoying the freedom of youth. The warm, sunny climate of Texas matched my bright enthusiasm for life. My future seemed full of fun, challenges and new discoveries. That August morning, all my optimism vanished and was replaced by the darkness of fear, anger, confusion, self-destruction, shame and guilt of victimhood as I entered a hallway that is every woman's nightmare.

Many times, over many years, I wished I'd fought harder, plunged the knife into that man's side when I had the chance, or died defending myself rather than live with the loss of my innocence and my dreams. My greatest fear became the thought of it happening to one of my sisters, my mom, or a relative or friend. And anger permeated every cell of my body, every thought, every gesture.

The first year I couldn't sleep during the darkness of each night and could not focus on anything. I spent four months wandering to and from relatives' homes across the country, trying to outrun and drink away flashbacks and the separation I felt. Doors appeared in that hallway from time to time, but when I went through one of them, it just seemed to lead into another hallway.

I spiraled into numbing my pain with drugs, alcohol, and beginning and ending relationships. I continued to wander from state to state, city to city, job to job, college to college, lover to lover, and identity to identity. My anger grew, and I came to believe it was me against the whole world. And it was me alone; no God, no love, no hope of hope. I mourned my lost innocence, I believed I was damaged goods and finally decided just to get over it already . . . move on, push it down, it's no big deal, that was the past, who cares?

Life goes on, hallway or no hallway, healed or

wounded, acceptance or not. I lived as a victim, but that became my business and nobody else's.

I hated men; I hated society for accepting men's violations and abuse of women, children and each other, and I hated myself for even caring about injustice. I just about hated myself into death. Suicide was an option for a very long time, especially after sobering up.

Living that angry, with all the shame and guilt and separateness, prevented any attachments to anyone or anything. My trust in the Universe/God had been stolen from me, and no matter how much information I acquired about all the other women throughout history who had lived through—and were living with—being raped, I still felt dirty, ruined and alone.

Sobriety saved my life, but my heart was still slammed shut, and I had carefully over time constructed a fortress of protection between me and others.

Some of the barricades across those hallway doors did crumble and fall as I worked the 12 Steps of AA and cautiously let AA's love me. Spirit guided me into life without alcohol and drugs, but I wasn't going to get carried away with love or commitment or 'brotherhood' or trust or dreams—those things could be snatched away!

I was still one pissed-off woman, and that anger insured that others would stay away from me. But my body, mind and soul grew stronger one day at a time, and I began to feel useful, and I began to want to feel whole. Which meant facing my anger and learning to trust and love—not just to love others but love myself, too, and harder still, allow others to love me.

A therapist gently convinced me to join a group of women survivors of sexual abuse, and I absolutely knew it was time to take action and take responsibility for healing my long-festering wounds. As a way of introduction to those five women, we all took a session to share our stories. My turn came, and for the very first time ever, I verbalized all the details of my rape—held back nothing. (In past renditions I'd held back as an attempt to protect the listener.) I shared the pain, physical and emotional, the anger, the hopelessness, the belief of separateness, the self-loathing.

And the deepest, closest-kept secret: a second rape within months of the first.

I had for years blamed myself for that second rape because I was drunk (again), in a place I shouldn't have been, alone and an easy target after a "mickey" was slipped into my drink. I also felt horrid about not attempting to report that one, especially since I had evidence the guy was a serial rapist. (That still haunts me at times.)

Step Five in the 12 Steps of AA says that we "Admitted to God, to ourselves and to another human being the exact nature of our wrongs." After I went through an honest and thorough Fifth Step, I began to free myself from the past, to feel less isolated, to feel forgiven no matter what I had done and to become more aware of who I was. To feel peace and a sense of oneness with God and with other human beings.

I gained the awareness that I was the one who'd kept me locked in that hallway all those years. By not forgiving myself and hanging onto my shame, guilt and anger, I had actually blocked the doors that led out.

The rapists were sick, wrong and long-since forgiven; the callous cops; the sleazy defense lawyer; the unjust justice system; the invasive medical treatment; the knife wounds on my side; the shattered confidence and dreams had all faded into the hallway corners and shadows. It was my belief—the belief that I didn't deserve to be treated with love and compassion—that had held me captive.

My heart opened ever so slightly and has yet to do anything except open wider and wider. Self-forgiveness was the key to unlocking the door leading out of the victim's hallway. God and love once again could move in, out and through me.

4 Doors That Close Slowly

Sometimes a door creaks shut for years. Maybe you decide to retire, or your child is about to leave home. Maybe a loved one is dying.

This hallway has a dog-leg. First, there's a prolonged period of anticipation when you know a door is closing. Then after it finally shuts, you're in a second hallway where you have to adjust to the change.

Even though you knew it was coming, this hallway may be no less challenging than those that are a surprise.

THE EMPTY NEST HALLWAY

Parents know from the day a child is born that, if all goes well, their baby will grow up and leave home. Some parents celebrate their freedom when it happens; other parents aren't sure what to do with themselves.

Laura Shepard began dreading her empty nest two years before her son finished high school.

"As he started to get older, the realization was hitting that in two years, he's going to go off to college, and everything's going to be different."

His last two Christmases, his last two birthdays. "I

was dwelling on all the *lasts* of his living in this house. And seeing him every day, it was excruciating, the thought that Robert's not going to be in the house anymore."

Robert, vaguely aware of his mom's emotions, was busy being a teenager, seeing friends, checking out colleges. Laura knew her life was good, but she was trapped in her sad thoughts. "I created misery in my brain," she confessed.

Robert eventually graduated and happily left home for his dad's alma mater 2,000 miles away.

"Once it happened and he actually left, it wasn't as horrible as the two years of anticipating his leaving," Laura said. "Now in retrospect, of course, I have regrets that I didn't enjoy the last two years, I didn't stay in the moment and be present for his last two years in the house. I was grieving his leaving. I was more focused on the absence of him that was to come.

"But what I've learned from that whole miserable anticipation of the hallway is how ridiculous it was and what a waste of time it was."

She's grateful for a second chance with her younger daughter. "I know it's limited time. Even when I get sick of driving her to school, I remember this isn't forever, and this is my time with her now. It was a huge lesson that I learned the hard way."

One common gift of the hallway is learning to appreciate the present moment, just as it is.

THE RETIREMENT HALLWAY

Dr. Sue Carpenter—"Doc" to her friends—had no idea retiring would be so difficult. She was 70 when she decided to leave her job as a school psychologist, and she gave a year's notice. A miserable year, as it turned out.

"I would literally bury myself in my office and do research and writing. I hid, basically," she said.

"I knew I was coming toward the end, and I think I was already beginning the grieving of that. You do withdraw, you close in, you encapsulate yourself a little bit. I had to protect my heart."

She knew retiring was the right thing to do. "I was at the time, I was at the place, and it was time to say goodbye. And that was the hard part—saying goodbye to so many years. And waking up one morning and knowing, 'I don't have to go anywhere today. I don't have to do anything today. Oh. Now what?'

"I knew it was coming, but I didn't know how great a hit it was going to be to my identity. For me, if your life has been defined not by who you are but by what you do, you press up really hard against that as a deep, deep loss.

"Then you have to go through the process of redefinition and re-identifying, and that has taken me a while. I've had to look at *Who am I? What am I? What do I have to offer?*"

Doc Sue went through two years of deep mourning. Her daughter urged her to become active, get out of the house. But Doc Sue walked blindly through some of her days, aimless, searching for a door.

"I waited. I'd honor the grieving. I knew I was

walking through the dark night of the soul, and I simply had to wait it out.

"But during that time, I was in a process of discovery. What else am I interested in, what else do I like to do, how can I make the shift from being gainfully employed to just being gainful? That was a hard thing, because all my life, whatever I did, I did to get money. Now whatever I do, I do to nourish the soul of somebody else or to nourish mine, and there's no dollar attached to that."

In retirement, Doc Sue is a chiropractor who practices two days a week. She's also a photographer, writer and artist who describes herself as a crone, a wise woman.

The work-for-money world looks frenetic to her now, with people moving and talking too fast. She watches her adult children absorbed in their jobs, sometimes missing life to make a living.

"I am absolutely delighting now in the time I have that is more gentle, more attentive, more deliberate, way more spiritual because I don't have the distraction I used to have," she said. "Tomorrow I start volunteering at a stable that does therapeutic riding for people who are handicapped. I'm so excited I can hardly stand it."

Rediscover, redefine and re-emerge, she said.

Doc Sue told me she had driven to a favorite park for our scheduled telephone interview, and she was viewing the scene as we talked. It was not gray and cold as one might expect in a Chicago winter. The land was fallow and quiet, she said. The birds were still in evidence. Doc Sue drank it in as she reflected on this late period of her life.

"The beauty of the season is all about me."

BITS OF WISDOM

* You might hear a door creaking shut for years before you enter the hallway.
* An empty nest, retirement or the final illness of a loved one are long hallways of anticipation that lead to hallways of adjustment.
* Bask in today.
* You are being offered an opportunity to redefine your life.
* Don't miss the present moment just because you know the end is coming.
* The beauty of the season is all about you.

THIS PRAYER IS FOR YOU

No matter how long you anticipated this change, you might not feel prepared for it now. You are going through something new and different, and it brings opportunities for you to design your life anew.

In this moment of inner silence, immerse yourself in the divine love that surrounds you. You are not alone, no matter what has changed in your life. You are simply continuing your human journey on a path that has turned a corner.

As you move forward, you will discover strength you did not know you had, and you will tap into your creativity. You will compose your life under new circumstances.

You cannot make a mistake, only learn and grow.

Today you might see just a step or two ahead on the path. But know that the journey before you leads to your highest good.

5 Choosing the Hallway

The most frightening and exhilarating hallways might be those we choose ourselves. We close the door on our own jobs, marriages, friendships or lifestyles and move toward something new.

Some doors need to be closed. Nothing lasts forever—no relationship, no job, no project. Even those that don't end will change, and you might need time to carve a new path.

Most people fear change, of course, and many try to avoid it. The uncertainty, the loneliness. Maybe a bad relationship is better than none. Maybe a safe job is more practical than following your bliss.

But at some point, for nearly everyone, life will call you higher and further than you thought you could go, and you will risk a journey through the hallway to get there.

MY OWN HALLWAY

I am one of many who deliberately closed a door and purposefully moved into a period of transition and uncertainty. After working for 22 years, I left my career as a newspaper reporter to become a minister.

The greatest courage was required at the beginning.

I had been aware for about three years that I didn't want to spend the rest of my life in journalism, but I had no idea what else to do. I started attending church—to fill a spiritual emptiness that was part of turning 40, I thought—but I never connected church to my work.

The idea to study for ministry, when it came, seemed heaven-sent and crazy at the same time.

Me, a minister? I was nothing like the ministers of my childhood. They were men, to begin with, glad-handing, hale and hearty extroverts who wore white shoes and pompadours. I have since learned that ministers come in all personality types—studious intellectuals, shy recluses, touchy-feely earth mothers—but overcoming my own stereotype of what a minister should be took years, even after ordination. I felt like a fraud every time someone called me Reverend. Occasionally, I burst out laughing.

For the most part, friends and family were supportive of my career change. Except my mother.

"The salary! The prestige! You want to give all that up?" (Bless her heart, she must have thought my reporting career was in a league with Diane Sawyer's or Katie Couric's. Hardly.)

Her reaction reflected all the fears I didn't want to acknowledge: I was giving up security for the unknown, I might starve to death on a minister's salary, I would miss journalism, I would live a life of loss and regret, I was trading the cachet of covering presidential campaigns for—well, for God.

I was sure she was wrong, but I still remember lying

in bed at night with waves of fear crashing over me, mostly about money. What if I didn't have enough in my 401K to get through school? What if I never found a ministerial job that paid a living wage? What if I was, in fact, sorry? What if I hated ministry, or church people hated me? What if my spiritual beliefs were wrong? Was I just running away from my life?

Being accepted into seminary sent me into a tailspin of Am I Doing the Right Thing. I was single and free—no spouse, no kids, no mortgage to consider. A new start and fulfillment awaited. Still, there were nights when I could hardly breathe through the fear, much less pray.

I was relieved when classes finally began. Then one of the faculty said on the first day, "If you become a minister, you can expect to be out of your comfort zone for the rest of your life."

He was right. There has been no end to the growth opportunities.

YOU ASKED FOR IT

Maybe choosing to close a door in your own life won't require the same depth of adjustment, forgiveness, prayer and healing as the more sudden or tragic hallways. But it still can throw you into turmoil.

When I think about all those political campaigns I covered as a reporter, I see hallways. Running for office is a long, self-selected hallway for the candidates. The winner will open the door to a new job, new status, new visibility, whether local or national. The loser will go home to profound quiet, the phone no longer ringing, often in debt and out of work, feeling rejected and guilty for letting down so many supporters. Through months and sometimes years of campaigning, the future is unknown to the candidates, their families, staffs and supporters. They only know their lives will change, literally overnight, on a date certain. And they volunteered for this!

Choosing the hallway sometimes takes enormous courage at the same time it appears to be the only option. I think of a beautiful young woman in my church, the single mother of a toddler, who moved halfway across the country to go to graduate school, gambling that it would lead to a meaningful job. Such heroism is typical among those who are committed both to family and professional fulfillment. They choose hallway after hallway.

Some changes are carefully considered in advance. You make lists of pros and cons, you do the math to see what you can afford, you consult with experts and friends about the best course of action.

Other times, choosing the hallway is like jumping off a cliff.

A BUSINESS HALLWAY

Vickie was a manager in a camera store where she had worked for 23 years when technology overtook the industry. Fewer people were using film in cameras, and brick-and-mortar stores that sold cameras and developed photos were a dying business. She was told her responsibilities and her salary would be drastically downsized.

"Before I had a chance to think, the words just jumped out of my mouth: 'I am going to start my own business!'"

The people she had been working with at the camera store tried to talk her out of it.

"They told me how lucky I was, in this economy, to at least have a steady job with benefits. They told me to be grateful, and that I was taking a risk. (They now take full credit for pushing me out of the nest!)"

Vickie stepped into the hallway of uncertainty and closed the door behind her. The next door opened almost immediately—actually heavy oak double doors inside the credit union where she had banked for 20 years.

She stopped by one day to withdraw enough cash to buy her own business name.

"While waiting at the teller counter, I noticed a stairway off to the right that I hadn't noticed before. I asked the person at the counter where the stairs went, and she told me the second floor had been vacant for over 2 1/2 years, and she wished they could find a tenant."

At the top of the stairs, the double doors led to two offices and a kitchen. The former boardroom was perfect as a classroom. The credit union downstairs furnished Vickie's lobby and paid for security, utilities and the Internet. The vice president helped maintain her website. She was getting calls for business in less than a month, teaching classes even before she could post a calendar.

Her timing perfectly caught the wave from film to digital photography. Everyone needed to learn the new art—kids, adults of various skill levels, even professional photographers. She taught them all.

Vickie also began to apply the spiritual principles she had learned about living in an abundant universe, something we'll explore in Part Three. When she needed more income, someone sublet her classroom to teach business analysis to immigrants from India. When she needed to sell her house, someone from her church bought it.

"I know that whatever I need will be provided," Vickie now believes.

A REVERSE HALLWAY

Brooke had a dream wedding at a castle in the Scottish Highlands, surrounded by rolling hills with evergreens covered in snow. The dress, the caterers, the gowns for her mother and sister—everything was a fairy tale.

Except she didn't love him.

"I remember crying in the airport. All along, in the back of my mind, I knew this wasn't right, but I felt trapped.

"I knew I could never divorce someone, so I accepted it. I made the bed; I had to lie in it. I remember thinking those exact words. Most people saw this as an amazing day. To me, the door to my happiness was slamming shut."

Nearly two years later, Brooke found the courage to say she didn't want to be married anymore, and her young husband laughed with relief. They parted happily.

Brooke dutifully showed up for a divorce support group, but she found a bunch of weepy people watching a depressing video, and she feared her joy mocked their pain.

"These people were going through hell, their own

hallway. I felt like I was coming out of my hallway into a wonderful, bright world." She told the group leader she wouldn't be back.

"I moved into a cute, hip loft in downtown. I bought a zippy car, started grad school and returned to the theater. I even bought my own house.

"Anytime I ran into someone, they gave that sad look. 'How are you doing?' they'd ask with their heads cocked to the side. They felt so bad for me. I bounced back with 'Great! I've moved, I'm studying...' My excitement confused but pleased them."

She now compares the experience to looking in a mirror where everything is reversed.

"Most people would see my marriage as something wonderful, my divorce as something tragic, and my rebuilding as something painful I had to endure. But it was all a mirror. My [wedding] was a door closing, the marriage was the hallway to find my strength, and my divorce was the freedom to become myself again."

You close a door on the life you have known and choose to enter a hallway simply by the choices you make. The decisions that are questioned, even criticized, by others might be the best possible experiences you could create for yourself. No one knows the right doors to close or the right ones to open, except you.

BITS OF WISDOM

❋ You might purposefully close a door behind you and step into the hallway.

✳ Some doors need to be closed. Nothing lasts forever.

✳ Fear of the unknown can keep you stuck. Risk a journey through uncertainty if you are being called higher.

✳ If others object to your decision, they might be reflecting your own fears to you.

✳ Choosing change takes enormous courage, even when it looks like the only option.

✳ Whatever you need will be provided.

THIS PRAYER IS FOR YOU

So here you stand in a hallway of your own making.

This is the change you said you wanted, and now you are between what was familiar and whatever is yet to be. You might be surprised how frightened you are. You thought you were sure about your decision, and now, maybe not.

Remember, you were guided to do this. You chose this period of adjustment with the goal of improving your life. And your life is a universal project, attended by angels and guides and the love of a divine Presence that dwells within you.

No matter what you imagine your future holds, it will be even better. It will be exactly what you need for your highest growth and greater good. Keep moving forward.

6 Inner Hallways

Some hallways are invisible to other people. You enter them in silence and open doors only you can reach.

Many such hallways are spiritual, when your seeking is entirely within yourself. The changes these hallways bring about might not be visible but are profound nonetheless.

Inner hallways are common to middle age, when many of us begin to fill holes inside us after being busy for years with school, marriage, kids and work. When I was turning 40, I realized I had followed my life script and checked most of the boxes under the heading of Adult Success, but I still came up empty. I wondered why I was on the planet.

Now a younger generation is searching for meaning, too. I'm happy to see 20- and 30-somethings who already know money is not the ultimate goal.

Questions of meaning, purpose and identity push us into inner hallways, which are difficult to describe. How exactly can you explain to someone the important changes that are taking place, when all the action is deep within you?

This process of growth and change, releasing and deepening—even the purification of a dark night of the soul—takes time to recognize, much less put into words. This isn't small talk for a dinner party!

The term "dark night of the soul" is tossed around to describe any period of emotional pain, but in fact, it is a very specific experience when all connection with the divine seems lost. Prayers dry up, meditation feels useless and ritual becomes empty. Nothing works anymore. God seems nowhere to be found. Endless wilderness.

The concept stems from a poem by St. John of the Cross, a 16th century Spanish monk, who said the dark night finally gives way to the perfect brilliance of the divine. It is an excruciating experience, rare and intense, and ultimately so exquisite that remaining in the ordinary world is a challenge thereafter. Most of us cannot imagine this annihilation of self, and most of us will not experience it in a lifetime.

More commonly, you and I will go through spiritual dry spells for a while. A door closes on the comfortable way we viewed the world, how it works and our place in it. Even if our previous experience did not include God or any spiritual practice, something invisible that nurtured us seems to have vanished. The feeling is bereft, confused, hopeless and a little panicky. Or at the very least, useless and burned out. Blah.

But these wilderness periods lead to a new level of spiritual understanding. They spiral into brighter, clearer light than we had known before. We might not turn into ecstatic mystics, in love with the Beloved, but we will sense a stronger connection to All That Is.

Inner hallways might not appear dramatic, but they can bring about shifts in consciousness that change your understanding of your very existence.

TALKING TO A TREE

Dottie was approaching 65 when she decided to live in an awareness of *being* rather than the busyness of *doing*.

She had had long, successful careers in corporations and as an entrepreneur. She had been on the vanguard of women in business and also had carried out the endless To Do list of a wife and mother. She was exhausted.

"How do I leave behind 60-plus years of conditioning as a doer? What does it mean to have my *doing* driven by who I am *being*? I felt vulnerable and exposed in not knowing what to *do*. The first light bulb that went off suggested that I needed to figure out who I wanted to *be*."

For her inner journey, Dottie engaged a Zen priest as a coach to provide support and direction. With his help, she began an intentional meditation practice that grew from about 60 seconds a day to 60 minutes.

"Eventually I discovered that the things I found myself 'doing' seemed to feel different from before. There was a renewed energy, rather than an exhaustive state, that seemed to spring from the things I was being directed to do."

Those of us who knew Dottie were amazed she could sit still long enough to meditate. But nothing surprised us more than the day this accomplished corporate executive and feminist pioneer, who had written books and been invited to speak all over the world, engaged in conversation with a tree.

Dottie was attending a weekend workshop in which one of the exercises was to take a walk and try to connect with something in nature.

"I found myself walking to a nearby park where I sat on a bench and wondered exactly what it meant to 'connect with something in nature.' My eyes were eventually drawn to a tree that seemed impervious to any and all things occurring around it: blowing winds, children running about, etc. The tree seemed to sit in quiet repose.

"Eventually I found myself asking the tree (not out loud, of course!) what it was doing. The immediate response that came back was this: 'I'm not doing anything; I'm being a tree.'

"This was a watershed moment for me. My job, it seemed, was to be Dottie, and I had the joy of defining who she is and living from that space."

ONLY LOVE

June said when she first heard the concept of the hallway, she felt as if she were living there all the time, unsure which door to open. So began her quest to answer the big question: Why am I here?

She wanted some grand life purpose!

"And then, one day it came... Love. Instead of being really big, it was just so simple. I am here to love.

"Not the romantic kind (although that's always nice), not the nurturing kind, but the unconditional kind. The kind that allows you to see through the human into the light that is inside of them. Since this revelation in my life, I have changed my whole outlook on life in general.

"This is why I tell you I love you every time I see you, why I hug with my heart energy everyone I see.

You have no idea how many people out there just need love. And the ones that don't think they need it, or don't want it, I just love them behind their backs. The energy is the same, and the effect is still the same. And I am really good at it!"

June now sees her love being passed on through her daughter to her grandchildren. And she finally sees love as a grand life purpose.

"I no longer feel it to be a small thing. I've seen how it changes people—the spark in their eyes when they feel that unconditional love energy from me. My gift is a special one for sure!"

Inner hallways lead to a new sense of who you are, not just what you do. Sometimes you won't even realize how much you have changed until you encounter an old situation and respond in a new way.

Elisabeth Kubler-Ross wrote, "People are like stained-glass windows. They sparkle and shine when the sun is out, but when the darkness sets in, their beauty is revealed only if there is a light from within."

BITS OF WISDOM

* An inner hallway may be invisible to others, but this passage is required to fill some emptiness in you.
* An inner hallway is a time of growth and transition, releasing and deepening.
* Most of us go through spiritual dry spells, when we feel disconnected and our practices don't seem to work anymore.

* Focus on your essential being. Who are you without your identity? Who are you if you do nothing but *be*?
* The spiritual wilderness often leads to a mountaintop.

THIS PRAYER IS FOR YOU

Divine restlessness tugs at your inner sleeve, demanding attention, prodding you toward change. No one can tell, just by looking, what you are going through. Maybe you can't even put it into words.

You are in a hallway leading from one part of your Self to the next. This is God at work in your life.

A door is waiting for your touch. You will find it. This restlessness is Life telling you that more is available. Your greater good awaits.

Just keep putting one foot in front of the other. You might be amazed where this hallway leads.

7 Endless Hallways

For many years, I assumed every hallway ended with a door that could be opened. Then I began to hear from people who feel trapped in endless hallways.

Someone in the family is mentally ill. A child is autistic or developmentally disabled. An illness is termed "degenerative." A spinal cord injury has paralyzed a body, or a brain injury has paralyzed a life.

A great many situations are not lethal. Instead, they are going to last forever. For the rest of your life and beyond. Your job is to deal with it. Every. Single. Day.

My heart breaks for you in these endless hallways. If you were caring for a dying parent, at least you would know the experience would eventually end. With a cancer diagnosis, you could always hope for remission or improvement. Hearts heal from divorce; jobs can be replaced.

But sometimes, life as you know it is altered forever by circumstances that will never change or improve. Your hallway appears to have no doors at all. More physical strength, emotional stamina, compassion and patience will be required of you than you ever imagined you could summon.

"HE'LL PROBABLY NEVER CHANGE"

When Sarah's son was small, the label applied to him was "borderline mentally retarded." He couldn't always control his behavior in school, needed special education classes and was depressed through high school.

"He's smart enough to know he's different," Sarah said. "People would make fun of him and take advantage of him."

As an adult, he was kicked out of a group home for smoking marijuana, so, now in his mid-30s, he lives at home with his mom and stepdad.

"He takes a lot of energy. You could tell him the same thing every day, and the next day you have to tell him again. 'Clean up after yourself, be sure you wash your hands, put away the food!'"

Sarah has lived with this long enough to be philosophical.

"I think the whole relationship with children is very organic. You kind of flow with it. And of course as a mother or father, you always want the best, and you always want to protect your children. I think we understand that he'll probably never change, and that's just who he is."

LIVING IN THE BUBBLE

Jean has experienced an endless hallway as a sibling. Now in her 60s, a large part of her life has been dominated by her sister Carol's developmental disabilities.

Looking back, Jean and her brother believe their

parents let Carol's differences take over their lives, that they gave her power to run the household. But what do you do with a child who has screaming meltdowns, who swings from good moods to bad without warning?

"I felt shamed," Jean told me. "I didn't understand it at the time, but there was a terrible sense of shame and inferiority, that we'd been marked, and this was like an open wound. We couldn't ever go out in public with my sister because she'd start screaming, she would do something inappropriate. Our relatives were put off by her—I recognize it now—because she was so out of control.

"We always had parties, birthday parties and picnics. But no one ever came around when there wasn't a party. No one ever said, 'How's Carol? Let me take her for the afternoon, or she can come over to my house.'

"They didn't know how to handle her. We didn't either."

Jean still remembers the useless and insensitive platitudes people offered her family.

Everything happens for a reason.

God doesn't give you anything you can't handle.

What doesn't kill you makes you stronger.

She heard them as glib excuses from people who refused to help. Jean wanted to scream at them: "We *can't* handle this! We're all depressed. The monster's in the hallway with us. We're functioning, (but) we're the walking wounded."

The family tiptoed on eggshells to keep from setting off Carol. Her parents even took turns going to Mass so one of them always could be at home with Carol.

"My sister became our identity. We lived in her bubble," Jean said.

Jean grew up and left home as soon as she could. "I figured if I didn't leave, I would end up committing suicide, which would be worse. What helped was leaving and realizing my life was bigger than my sister."

What also helped was finding a biblical answer to the question "why." This passage became Jean's life raft:

> His disciples asked him, "Rabbi, who sinned, this man or his parents, that he was born blind?" Jesus answered, "Neither this man nor his parents sinned; he was born blind so that God's works might be revealed in him." *(John 9:2-3 NRSV)*

"That Bible verse helped me realize this wasn't a judgment from God. That was a huge help. I didn't understand the mystery behind this, and maybe I wasn't meant to understand the mystery. But it wasn't that we had done something wrong or there was something wrong with us."

Carol was cared for at home until her mother was past 70, and she now lives in a group home where the staff is infinitely patient.

Her assessments say she "requires a lot of attention to prevent unacceptable behavior" such as fake crying, cursing and yelling. She talks about inappropriate subjects, invades others' personal space, drools and makes a mess eating.

Jean recently drove her middle-aged sister to a

weekend family cookout, and Carol started pulling Jean's hair while they were on the highway. Being around her is exhausting and always has been. And the family never talked about it, Jean said.

"We were all stuck in the hallway, and my sister locked us in."

I wish I had a solution for these seemingly endless hallways, wish I could open a magical doorway to a land where everything is perfect. On the other hand, how many people have learned and grown from these unexpected turns in life? How many said later it was a blessing they wouldn't have wanted to miss?

The only door out of an endless hallway has to be found within you. Not by pretending everything's fine when you want to scream, but by somehow finding acceptance and peace on more days than not. A shift in consciousness is the only way out.

As you continue to read about what to do in the hallway and how to move out of it, I expect the solutions found by others, such as prayer, forgiveness and acceptance, will be useful even if you can't hope for any change in your outer circumstances.

Jean has waited eagerly to share what she went through with her sister and wants to offer three suggestions that might help other families:

* "Forgive the people who say the terrible platitudes to us, because they have no idea."
* "We have to have respite. We have to have a life outside of being in the hallway."
* "Develop relationships with other family members outside the problem."

Maybe more help is available now, maybe families are more enlightened, maybe states provide better care with respite for caregivers. But these endless hallways, like every hallway, can only end within you.

BITS OF WISDOM

✳ The hallway might seem endless if your circumstances are unlikely to improve, but look for the light.
✳ Sometimes the door that opens will not lead to changed circumstances, but to peace with what is.
✳ The door out of an endless hallway has to be found within.
✳ You still have the power to create your life, right where you are, no matter what is around you.

THIS PRAYER IS FOR YOU

Turn within for a moment of peace. It's true, this isn't the life you planned or expected. You look at other people and wonder what it would be like to be normal. But your path is different.

Your path could be a special gift.

Consider: You are where you are supposed to be, and your life is unfolding as it was designed for you by your own soul, in oneness with a higher power who is with you at every step.

So take a deep breath and keep moving through this endless hallway. Trust your inner guidance. The doors you open along the way might not be visible to anyone else and might not change your circumstances. But you will know that something has shifted deep within you.

Day by day, you will feel more love, more peace and more understanding. And someday, gratitude. Yes, even for this.

8 Short Hallways

Once you recognize the hallway as a recurring event in your life, you can see it even in short episodes. Waiting to hear whether you will get the job. Waiting to hear whether they accept the offer on the house. Waiting to see whether the stick turns pink.

One of the most frequent and intense short hallways is waiting for the results of medical tests. Within days, you may find out whether life as you know it has changed dramatically or will continue as usual.

Our brains can imagine an untold number of awful scenarios during just a few days of uncertainty!

You might think a short hallway doesn't need all the spiritual work that is required in the longer ones, but a little prayer never hurt. Short hallways can be intense.

IS IT LEUKEMIA?

Marilyn Miller was 35 years old when her twin girls were born, a surprise and delight. They were nothing alike—dark-eyed Meredith weighed two pounds more than fair Megan—and the smaller baby struggled as she grew. She slept upright on Marilyn's chest to alleviate the pain of earaches, and she needed to be held nearly all the time.

"It seems as though we rocked 100,000 miles in that old brown, overstuffed rocker," Marilyn remembers.

Megan developed more slowly and learned to walk by bouncing on her tiptoes. The odd gait worried her grandmother, who begged for an examination. Marilyn finally took the toddler for a doctor visit, which included routine blood tests.

"The medical assistant had difficulty getting blood from the tiny finger. It seems she squeezed that little finger forever, with Megan screaming from the discomfort and fear of the moment. I was told to call the office in a couple of days for the lab results."

She got the news on a Friday. Little Megan's white blood cell count was high.

"Looks like we are dealing with some sort of leukemia," the doctor said. She recommended taking Megan to the big children's hospital for further testing. Right now. The lab would be closing for the weekend.

Marilyn rushed home to pick up Megan and drive to the hospital, wasting precious time in a phone booth (before the days of cell phones) trying to reach her husband at work. He met her at the hospital, but they were too late. Lab CLOSED.

"We all went home. We tried to keep Megan from knowing anything was wrong, but the atmosphere at our house was bleak. We cried. We called a few relatives. My heart broke as I watched my husband feed Megan red Jell-o and spinach leaves to try to build her blood. People visited as if there had already been a death.

"I prayed without ceasing. I rocked Megan all she

wanted, never worrying about what else I needed to be doing. I just held her and rocked her and wept silently. She looked up at me with all the innocence of her not quite 3 years of wisdom and asked, 'Mom, are there rocking chairs in heaven?' The lump in my throat felt as big as a walnut. I swallowed hard and told her, 'Yes. Yes, there are.'"

Marilyn called her pastor, but it was hours before he arrived. "I was hoping he would have the right words to make us feel better. (But) he didn't know God any better than I did. I had to find my own comfort from within."

It was a long, agonizing weekend.

Finally on Monday morning, they returned to the children's hospital for comparison blood tests.

"The technician was very fast and good with her finger stick. Megan did not even cry, and it was over in seconds, not minutes like the last time. Later, two doctors came in and said, 'She is fine. The blood count is normal.'

"I cried and held Megan close to me. She looked at me in amazement. She could not imagine what was wrong that Mom was crying out loud, moaning with relief.

"The technician re-entered the examination room and said, 'You do understand that your daughter is fine. The tests were okay. You don't have to cry.' I told her, 'I am crying for joy!'

"Later, the pediatrician told me that the medical assistant who drew the blood in her office had taken too long in getting the blood sample, and the blood had clotted, leaving the illusion of mostly white cells and a possible leukemia.

"The universe must have had something for us to learn that terrible weekend. I think the lesson for me was to find God and comfort within myself. No preacher, no husband or well-meaning friends could give me what I needed. We all went home and celebrated life and living and love. We had walked through the dark night of the soul and come out older and wiser and changed."

THE NINE-MONTH HALLWAY

When Santa (pronounced Sahn-tah, Spanish for *saint*) gave birth to a son, she and her husband hoped to have another child soon. Two kids, close together, and their family would be complete.

The first baby was just three months old when Santa was diagnosed with ovarian cancer.

If anyone can breeze through cancer, Santa did. She went into surgery knowing she could lose any chance of future child-bearing, but only one ovary was removed. She didn't need chemo or radiation. Another baby was still possible. Santa only had to wait. And wonder.

"There was no guarantee I would be able to get pregnant again," she said. "I didn't know if it would work, I didn't know whether my body would be an environment where it was possible anymore, or if it was a good choice. That waiting was really awful."

She knew if she stayed cancer-free for two years after the initial diagnosis, the chance of recurrence would drop dramatically. So she waited in the hallway until it felt safe to open a new door.

The two-year anniversary finally arrived, and Santa became pregnant immediately. When we talked, she was in a nine-month hallway, but Santa said she hardly noticed being pregnant, now that she had a toddler to chase after. Not like last time, when 40 weeks seemed an eternity to wait.

The hell in her hallway now was not waiting, she said. It was fear.

"So many things can go wrong, even though they mostly go right. It's hard not to think about the things that can go wrong, because you don't have control over it. It's Mother Nature. Babies come when they want to be born, even if it's too early. They may have different challenges when they're born. You never know what you're going to get."

She still has to visit the oncologist every few months to be scanned for cancer.

"Being able to practice releasing that fear and knowing everything's okay—even if it's just right now in this moment—I'm pregnant, I'm happy to be pregnant, to have this child. If tomorrow I'm not pregnant anymore, that's something I'll have to deal with. But for today, it's perfect.

"That's how I try to cope with being in that hallway— being present in every moment, day by day—being grateful for the child in my body today. Not knowing what the future has to hold but not focusing on that. Just focusing on right now."

She can't help but look forward, however. She sees her family camping and hiking together when the children are old enough. And she wants her body back! She grinned: "I'm lending my body to the pregnancy and to nursing for one or two years. I want to have my body belong to me again."

FREE FALLING

Less fearful and more amusing—well, for us—is the story of Ken's first attempt at skydiving. The lesson was a birthday gift from a former girlfriend. It turned into a short hallway to confront death.

"Everything about the appointed day was exciting and energizing. The skydiving lessons on the ground were easy and fun. Even watching the 30-minute video disclaimer that absolved the school of any liability seemed interesting," Ken wrote.

"When we finally took off in a beat-up old DC3—retrofitted to house large group formation dives—it all seemed great. I was sitting on the floor, and I couldn't see out the window. We finally got up to altitude and the drop zone. My instructor, now behind me and hooked onto my parachute harness, told me to stand up. Still couldn't see outside because there was a formation dive consisting of 22 jumpers in front of us, shuffling towards the back of the plane to make their exit.

"Just as the last of those formation jumpers left and I could see the door and what lay beyond it, I froze in resolute fear. Instantly the pilot announced over the intercom that we had passed the drop zone and had to go around in order to make another pass.

"That trip around and back to the drop zone was my hell in the hallway. Yes, I signed up. Yes, I initialed the legal documents. Yes, I wholeheartedly engrossed myself in the lessons—on the ground. It was my flippin' decision, for God's sake.

"But now I was definitely in a place where I didn't want to be. I certainly never thought it would create the sheer panic I now felt. The trip for the plane to circle around lasted for hours, or so it seemed. Nobody ever chickened out, they assured me.

"I turned and looked at the 30-something-year-old instructor attached to my harness, and I arrived at the realization that he didn't look like he wanted to die. He seemed intelligent and, I thought, smart enough to have checked the parachute packing that would ultimately allow us to make the trip from 12,500 feet to the ground in one piece. Wherever I was going, he had to follow. He was cool as ice.

"So I adopted that mindset. I figured that he knew what he was doing and that he really wanted to stay healthy. As we crouched down into the doorway to make our exit, all of the fear immediately left me. It was amazing. I was going to be with this guy, and this guy looked very confident about the whole thing.

"Out we went. Greatest thrill I have ever experienced. Eventually I made four more jumps, three as a solo diver. I experienced the same fear at altitude, made the same adjustments in my mind, intellectualized my way through it and thoroughly enjoyed the fruits of that exercise. I'd jump tomorrow if my wife would let me."

Ken and Marilyn had to draw from deep inner resources in a way that ultimately changed the way they viewed themselves. Santa deliberately appreciated every moment of her nine months until another healthy son was born. She and her family are thriving now.

Even short hallways can offer profound teachings.

BITS OF WISDOM

* ❋ Short hallways are periods of intense uncertainty that are resolved quickly, one way or another.
* ❋ A short hallway might require all the spiritual work of a long one. Just do it fast!
* ❋ If you are dreading a possible outcome, try to relax and be present for every good moment now.
* ❋ Draw from your own deep inner resources. You might be surprised what's within you.

THIS PRAYER IS FOR YOU

No matter the question you wait to have answered, keep breathing. Soon you will know what is next in your life, even though today, everything seems uncertain.

Many others have survived this short hallway while waiting for news, waiting for results, waiting to find out. You will know, and then you will be guided in your next steps.

You have a Presence within you that never leaves and can bring good from any event. Lean on it now.

And know you are loved. The prayers of everyone who has waited to learn what life holds for them are with you now.

9 Group Hallways

The mile-wide tornado rolled slowly across Joplin, Missouri, on a Sunday evening in May 2011, pulverizing everything in its path. Within minutes, 160 people were killed and more than a thousand injured.

Among the hundreds of homes, schools and businesses scraped off the earth in a six-mile trail of destruction was the Unity church, whose congregation was plunged into the hallway as a group. Their lives had changed irrevocably.

The sentimental idea that people band together after a disaster to serve and care for each other turned out to be only partly true.

"You saw the best of people, and you saw the absolute frickin' worst of people," said Rev. Kelly Isola, the minister who helped guide the church through recovery.

Imagine the thousands of hallways that are spawned by a natural disaster! The families of each person killed or injured are thrust into change. Families who lost their homes. Business owners and employees without offices or stores. Kids and teachers without schools. Doctors and nurses with no hospital. Each group touched by the event is in a hallway of loss and uncertainty.

Group hallways, whether they are dramatic or

mundane, are common to our experience but often unacknowledged during a transition. An office staff expecting layoffs to be announced, a ship's crew waiting for orders, a family trying to sell a house and move, a team waiting for a new coach—all are in group hallways. Then there are the cities, schools and businesses that have to pull together after natural disasters, mass shootings or other headline-making events.

When the future is uncertain for a whole group of people, their needs, desires and reactions to stress surface individually and collectively. It's a complicated juggling act for anyone who tries to help them.

As Kelly described her frazzled congregation, "For a year, it was like a bunch of sixth-graders."

HONORING THE LOSS

The little Unity church in Joplin had no minister when the tornado hit. Kelly, who had been a guest speaker some Sundays, was hired as the transitional minister to help the church clean up and begin to consider its future. She commuted weekly from Kansas City, 150 miles north, for three years.

As individuals, most of the 50 church congregants were lucky. Only a few had significant property damage; none of their group was killed. But friends were lost, jobs were lost, a hospital and the high school were demolished. Everything familiar about the town had changed.

Kelly did her share of comforting people about their myriad losses, including their church building, but some wanted to skip straight to positive thinking and pull themselves up by the bootstraps. She urged them to slow down and face the enormity of what had happened before they launched into the restoration phase.

Kelly asked the congregation to inspect the devastation on the church site and honor what had been lost. The children's classrooms, the musical instruments, the office computers, the new stained glass window. Everything that had made the church *theirs* was gone.

They marveled at the few items that survived. A set of four little bells they never used. Some candle holders. Half a pew with envelopes still tucked neatly in the back pockets. Stacks of outdated and unused hymnals that the church had hoped to get rid of lay intact within the wreckage.

Clean-up is much too simple a concept for what had to happen in the ensuing months—physically, emotionally and spiritually—to rebuild from the inside out. Kelly said she and the church members worked to find a balance in retrieving the best parts of the past, planning the future and dealing with the reality of now.

Finding a new church home turned out to be the easy part. It took nine months to buy and move into a 100-year-old historic church building that had survived the storm.

The more difficult project was addressing the conflicts that already had been simmering in the congregation, problems that had never been named or faced. Conflict is not uncommon among church members. But when the church building in Joplin blew away, everything inside was revealed.

"I've heard from more than one person—never publicly but one-on-one—have said to me that having the church destroyed was a blessing," Kelly said, "because there was so much stagnant, shadow energy in the church that maybe this was the only way to for it to be blown away. It blew out a lot of *ick*. It gave them the capacity to look back and see how dysfunctional they had been, how unhealthy."

There was so much to deal with in Joplin, sometimes emotions came out sideways. If congregants sent each other stinging emails or bickered about whether the chairs should face this way or that, Kelly knew they were yearning for a sense of safety and predictability.

When some expressed anger at God, others sometimes shut them down, chirping that God had a plan, everything was in divine order and the Lord would provide. Kelly saw it as a childlike attempt to avoid pain, pretending everything's fine.

"I never disagreed, but I would ask them, 'What if God didn't have a plan? What if you're the one divinely ordering the plan?'"

She tried to teach them that tension and disagreement are okay, that plowing through heated discussions can be healthy and creative. She wanted them to stay present to whatever they were feeling, even when it was uncomfortable. And she constantly listened for the need beneath their words.

"(Saying) 'I can't believe God let this happen' really isn't about God," she said. "They're angry, and they're hurt, and the brain wants to fill in the blanks and understand. They're wanting to know that, right here and now, they can be cared for and there's something good."

CREATING ANEW

Rather than reach into the past and try to rebuild everything the way it used to be, Kelly created a new routine for Sunday services. She even found a way to incorporate the four little bells that had survived.

At a deeper level, she tried to help the congregants look at unconscious, unexamined assumptions about themselves, God, church and how they related to each other.

"Everything's been taken away, so who do you want to be? How do you want to be? You get to decide right now. It's not just rebuilding. It's a clean slate."

The Latin roots of the word *compassion* mean "to suffer with." Kelly said she couldn't lead or teach the congregation until the individuals knew she truly understood their sadness, pain and anger.

"Even if they're angry at *you*, it's an invitation to connect. They just don't know how. They want to belong and know they're loved.

"Love first, teach second."

So how does any group of people move through a hallway together, even if it's not a full-scale disaster?

As you will read throughout this book, the specific circumstances of transition are secondary to the spiritual work that always needs to be done.

In group hallways, the work may be individual *and* collective, organizational *and* psychological. The same steps through the hallway that are taken by individuals also are useful for groups: acceptance, surrender, forgiveness, prayer and responsibility. More on each of these in Part Two.

I recognize that some organizations won't talk out loud about spirituality, although I continually find people in the workplace are more receptive than I expected. And of course, individuals may pursue the spiritual gifts of the hallway on their own, praying or forgiving as needed regarding their group's situation.

Ideally, leaders will be sensitive to group dynamics during transition. As Kelly learned, empathizing with the chaotic emotions can help. Once people feel understood, they may consider what they want for the future and begin to open doors, just as the Joplin congregation contemplated *who* and *how* it wanted to be going forward.

In that sense, every hallway offers a clean slate.

BITS OF WISDOM

✳ Some journeys through the hallway affect an entire group—a family, office, school, town or country.

✳ Slow down and face what has happened before you skip to positive thinking or forgiveness.

✳ A group hallway might intensify conflicts that already existed and reveal problems that were unacknowledged.

✳ Discord is only a longing for order and a return to normalcy.

✳ When life as you knew it is gone, you have a chance to decide who you want to be now, as an individual or a group.

THIS PRAYER IS FOR YOU

So here you are in a crowded hallway, anticipating with others what might happen next, waiting to know your mutual fate.

Close your eyes and ask yourself silently: What is mine to do? How can I best serve others as we traverse this time of uncertainty? How can we take every opportunity now to change for the better, individually and together?

Alone and quiet, feel your connection with these other people. You are one, each a part of the one Spirit, each an expression of the divine. You are joined at the heart.

You have been offered this period of time for reflection, clarity and deciding what you seek to create. Your group energy is powerful. Your desires vibrate through the universe. And you are drawing to you now exactly what is best for each of you and all of you.

10 Feelings in the Hallway

My friend Cherie has spent the past few years taking care of her husband's aging parents. She has organized her life around their medical procedures and lost sleep on the nights they were sick or confused or scared. Before her father-in-law died, hallucinations made him even more difficult to manage.

Finally one day, she said out loud: "I hate this!"

And she felt so much better.

She didn't hate the in-laws and, in the long run, she was doing what she wanted to do, to be of service. But it was tiresome and frustrating. It was painful to watch their decline and was inconvenient to put her life on hold indefinitely. Some days she hated it.

The point is, she said so!

Whatever your hallway, whatever the circumstances or duration of the change going on in your life, feel it. Feel sad, mad, hurt, put-upon, victimized—your feelings don't have to be pretty or logical or justifiable. They're just feelings.

But don't ignore them. I have come to believe feelings clamor for attention like small children and are soothed by acknowledgment. Feel them now, or dredge them up in therapy years from now.

Before we undertake the work of the hallway in Part Two, I want to be clear about just how bad it can feel. And encourage you to feel it anyway.

So many of our problems are created by our efforts to avoid feeling. Think of all the methods we use to numb ourselves: alcohol and drugs, of course, but also food, television, sports, working too hard, sometimes having affairs, sometimes flat-out denial. ("I am NOT ANGRY!")

Then, too, many of us on a spiritual path, who desire to live in higher consciousness and engage the world with love, try not to be human, not to feel and not to desire. We want to go with the flow and transcend any problem. We breathe and *Om* our way through life while neglecting to howl in pain every now and then.

Burying feelings in spirituality is no different from distracting ourselves with busyness or addictions or keeping a stiff upper lip. Why bother to be on earth if only to avoid the human experience?

Sometimes I think we try not to feel because we judge our feelings so harshly. In other words, I experience a feeling, then I judge myself for feeling it. Like this:

I'm sad, but I should be over this by now. I'm so weak!

I'm angry, but I'm probably being unfair. I'm a terrible person!

I hate this situation, but I feel guilty and ashamed of myself for being so petty and selfish and—well, you see how we judge ourselves? No wonder we don't want to feel anything! We feel bad about feeling bad.

Sometimes, too, old worn-out feelings are the last tie we have to a person or a particular time of life.

If I'm not angry with my ex, then he's truly gone forever.

If I stop telling my story of childhood abuse, then I have to take responsibility for who I am now.

One of the things I admire about people recovering in 12-step programs is that they learn how to sit in discomfort. Addiction numbed their feelings, but now they are stark, raving sober, facing life raw. It's not easy to be in pain without doing anything about it. Simply to *feel.*

THIS FIRE OF GRIEF

Mirabai Starr is an intriguing spiritual author whose first book was about St. John of the Cross. She translated his timeless poem and commentary from the antiquated Spanish and offered her own interpretation of his message of transformation.

Just after her shiny new copies of *Dark Night of the Soul* arrived at her home by UPS—a day of celebration for most authors—the police came to her door to say her 14-year-old daughter Jenny had been killed in a car accident.

Starr said she entered a time of "radical unknowingness"—the worst hallway imaginable—yet determined she would experience the horrendous emotional aftermath no matter how painful her feelings became. She vowed to her daughter: "I am going to honor you by not turning away from this fire of grief."

She was wracked with remorse and terrible guilt as a mother, but she leaned into the pain a hundred times a day. She had to "drop all expectations and ideas about what is natural and appropriate in this life. To face the impossible and not only allow it to be true, but to give thanks in all things," she wrote.

"To praise God for all of it. The sweet and easy moments when Divine love pours inexplicably into the broken heart like warm honey into a cup of tea. And the far more common moments of unspeakable agony when I realize yet again that my brilliant daughter will not grow up into the healer she had envisioned herself to be, that the girl would never finish blossoming into the woman she was becoming, that the difficult and fascinating personality that was my Jenny had been snuffed out like a flame, plunging my own life into darkness. To give thanks for those moments, too."

This quality of gratitude is beyond and so much deeper than positive thinking. This is opening to whatever life has to offer in its full spectrum of pain and sweetness. A spiritual being having a human experience is, by design, going to experience emotion. Otherwise we stifle our human opportunities and lose the spiritual understanding we came to earth to find.

SURPRISING FEELINGS

When you are faced with knowing life will never be the same, it's important to know that your feelings might not be what you expect.

Remember Ken, who told the story in Chapter 8 about waiting to parachute out of an airplane? A few years ago, he noticed tremors in his right arm and went to see a neurologist.

"The minute he saw me walk—he was coming up the hall to meet me in the hospitality area—he said, 'I'm doctor So-and-So, you've got Parkinson's.' Diagnosed me from 10 feet away."

Parkinson's is a degenerative disease of the nervous system with no cure.

When I talked to Ken, I did exactly what I know better than to do: I tried to make him a victim. I suggested he might be lying awake nights, wondering just how awful the Parkinson's could become, how dramatically his body might deteriorate.

Nope, Ken said, he worries about losing his house.

"I wake up every day at 4 o'clock in the morning thinking about how we can get more money in."

Ken is a muralist who is no longer safe on a ladder or scaffolding. He is a professional composer—songs, movie scores—who can no longer move his fingers on a keyboard. "My hands are like paddles."

He has worked for years on a musical he would love to see on Broadway. The script and Ken's music have received rave reviews from those privy to them, and producers on both coasts have looked for investors. But none of that has translated into income.

"I'm guessing if I get the financial problem solved, I may be worried about the Parkinson's. It's with me every minute. You have to stay aware of it."

He enunciated carefully in order to be understood. Speech problems affect nearly every Parkinson's patient. Ken said he also is embarrassed sometimes to stumble like a drunk in public.

"I don't have any shaking going on. I do fall down if I don't pay attention. I forget words, I mumble. I'm hesitant going through doorways—my feet just don't work."

Parkinson's is unpredictable and different in each person. Ken is doing everything he can to forestall deterioration—walking, swimming, even dancing; speech therapy, yelling exercises and singing in two choirs. Singing is great for his voice, but standing on the choir risers is dicey.

"I've got two guys on either side of me who pay very close attention to me, because I get very wobbly and could go down." In one of his choirs, every singer has Parkinson's.

This is the kind of hallway that doesn't have desirable doors to open. The best Ken can hope for physically is to minimize the impairment. Long-term illness is primarily an inner hallway, perhaps with openings to acceptance or peace, but not to permanent recovery.

I wondered about the effects on Ken's self-image or self-esteem, his willingness to face the world or even to keep living.

"There's a great deal of depression that goes along with this, and learning how to handle that is one of the tricks," he said. "There are times when I'm severely depressed, and you just have to fight your way through those things."

Hallways have varying degrees of emotional upheaval. What they all have in common is periods of uncertainty with little to do but *feel* whatever comes up on a given day.

I offer one more caution about feelings: No comparisons! It's not about the drama. The cause of your hallway does not determine the depth of your feelings.

Of course those who survive natural disasters or

debilitating diagnoses are thrust into long, difficult periods of recovery and recalibration in their lives. But there is no sweepstakes in suffering. Please don't compare your circumstances or your pain to anyone else's. Feel whatever you feel.

The work of the hallway is deeply personal and ultimately spiritual. We turn to that work now.

Wait

and see what comes

to fill

the gaping hole

in your chest.

Wait with your hands open

to receive what could never come

except to what is empty

and hollow.

—*Jan Richardson, from her blessing,*
"Stay"
janrichardson.com

BITS OF WISDOM

❋ Feelings clamor for attention and are soothed by acknowledgement.

* Feel your feelings now or dredge them up in therapy years from now.
* Spirituality does not exempt you from pain. Being spiritual is not the opposite of being human.
* Why bother to be on earth if only to avoid the human experience?
* Learn how to sit in discomfort. Lean into the pain. Do not turn away from the fire of grief.
* Open to life's full spectrum of pain and sweetness, and practice being grateful for all of it.

THIS PRAYER IS FOR YOU

This might be the worst, most painful period of your life. It might hurt to wake up and hurt to breathe. The fear, the grief, the anger may be overpowering at times.

Breathe now. Cry anytime. Let the feelings wash over you in waves. Feel them as they come to pass, because they will pass. Feelings only want to be felt. Give them their due, honor their power and let them move on.

You are enfolded in the arms of God, who weeps with you but knows your strength.

Even if you feel as if no one can possibly understand what you are going through, you are surrounded by the spirits of all those who have endured unspeakable pain, and you are uplifted by their love. You are a child of God who is loved beyond measure—yes, even in this.

It won't always hurt this much.

Part Two

The Work of the Hallway

Above all, trust in the slow work of God. We are quite naturally impatient in everything to reach the end without delay. We should like to skip the intermediate stages. We are impatient of being on the way to something unknown, something new. Yet it is the law of all progress that is made by passing through some stages of instability and that may take a very long time. And so I think it is with you. Your ideas mature gradually. Let them grow. Let them shape themselves without undue haste. Do not try to force them on, as though you could be today what time—that is to say, grace—and circumstances acting on your own good will, will make you tomorrow. Only God could say what this new Spirit gradually forming in you will be. Give our Lord the benefit of believing that his hand is leading you, and accept the anxiety of feeling yourself in suspense and incomplete.

—Pierre Teilhard de Chardin

11 What Now?

Some of the greatest pain I've experienced in life has come from sticking my foot into a closing door, hoping to avoid the inevitable. I've screamed and cried and pounded on the door, trying to keep it open. I've sobbed and cursed when the door was locked tight behind me, even when I knew its closing was for the best.

Many of us arrive in the hallway wounded and exhausted. It's tempting to pout, to review the story *ad nauseam* or to take on Victim as an identity.

We might spend hours, days, sometimes years in self-recrimination and second-guessing.

* Did I make the right end-of-life decisions for my parents or spouse?
* How could I have been so stupid in love? Why did I believe all the lies?
* Why didn't I see this layoff coming?
* Why wasn't I more careful with money?
* How could I have been a better parent?
* Why didn't I take care of my health?
* And some might ask, How could God let this happen?

We are, of course, creating our own hell in the hallway, taking a difficult situation and making it worse with our thoughts. But before we can begin any spiritual work, much less open a new door, we have to acknowledge and accept where we are.

Oh. I'm in the hallway. Like it or not, a door has closed, and the next has not yet opened.

So begins a journey through uncertainty. At times, it might seem as if the darkness will never end.

THE FIRST REACTION

I sat on the sofa next to Ed, a favorite church congregant who was being treated for cancer, and listened to him quote the oncologist.

"The five-year survival rate isn't very good."

Ed talked about his fear, his anger, his disappointment. He wondered whether living an extra year or two would be worth going through a second round of radiation and chemotherapy. He worried about his wife's finances after he was gone. So much uncertainty, so many decisions, so much emotion, and no clear way forward.

In my mind, I heard a door slam. Ed had been shoved into the hallway when he heard this latest diagnosis, and he experienced the emotional flood that often accompanies bad news. Or as he put it, "I felt like the whole world just sat on my head."

The prisoners of war in Vietnam had a name for it: prison thinking. It started the same way for everyone who was thrown into the Hanoi Hilton. Surprise, panic, blame and self-pity. The men who couldn't pull out of hopelessness died. The rest of them coached each other in how to think and what to expect.

Finding yourself in the hallway can feel like an immersion in flames, a slap in the face or a slow dawning. It might take time even to recognize where you are. *Oh, this isn't a dream. She really did leave. He really did die. They laid me off. There's no going back—that door has closed. What now?*

The most immediate experience of the hallway is grief. You have lost something—a person, a job, a way of life, a way of looking at the world. Whether a door was closed by . . .

death . . .

divorce . . .

illness . . .

bankruptcy or foreclosure . . .

work ending . . .

children growing . . .

whether you lost everything in a tornado, flood, hurricane, fire . . .

whether you knew change was coming or not . . .

even if you deliberately chose the change . . .

You are grieving a loss.

THE GIFTS ARE SPIRITUAL

The work of the hallway is not to fix a specific problem—heal a broken heart, struggle through an illness or emerge from bankruptcy. The work of the hallway is to meet the spiritual challenges that all life transitions have in common, to move consciously through a period of change and to milk it for any divine lessons and soul's growth it has to offer. That's what subsequent chapters are about.

Some life changes require immediate action. You might need to go into treatment or seek another job right away. Your actions will be tailored to your individual situation, but this book is not about addressing the events that put you in the hallway. Those circumstances will be different for everyone.

Whenever I speak about Hell in the Hallway, I am bombarded afterwards with people who want to tell me their stories. I love to hear them; obviously, I am a collector of hallway triumphs. But one or two people will chide me: "I kept waiting for you to talk about MY situation." Then they tell me their circumstances in minute detail.

Sometimes I want to take them gently by the shoulders and say, "It's not about the story. I'm not trying to cover every difficulty that might show up in your life. I'm offering spiritual principles to help you through *any* situation."

We will talk about those principles in the coming chapters. Meanwhile, I leave up to you the mechanics of treating your individual circumstances. Much has been written about recovering from loss—books with themes of how-to, self-help and why bad things happen. Some are psychological, some practical. You can find books about death, divorce, surviving illness, dealing with financial issues or parenting—whatever you are facing.

Find a therapist or doctor or shaman; learn to meditate or exercise; go away alone for a while or seek out people and parties. Find any teachers and tools that help you stay conscious as you move through this time of uncertainty.

Those outer, physical activities are good and necessary

But the real purpose and gifts of the hallway are for your spirit, no matter what has happened in your life. You have an opportunity to engage more deeply with the divine.

You are not here by accident. Even if you are convinced you are nothing but an innocent victim, and even if, at this point, you see no earthly reason why you need this experience, it might turn out to be the greatest blessing of your life. It can be redeemed for good. Whatever has happened is serving your life's purpose.

SOME INITIAL ADVICE

Before we wade into the deep work of the hallway, let me offer two initial bits of wisdom:

1. Let other people support you on this journey
2. Don't rush to find a way out

First, other people. You may be bombarded with advice from friends. You're likely to be smothered in sympathy, whether you're experiencing death or birth, love or loss, problems with money or family or health.

Let those people love you, tend your wounds, bring you tea. But pay attention to the attitude behind the actions. They might see you as a "poor thing" or paint you as a victim. As good as that can feel at first, being a long-term supplicant will not serve you.

I have friends who support me in two different ways. I call certain ones when I want sympathy and hand-holding, when I want to be assured I was right and the other person was wrong, or I want to be told that life is tough and I'm allowed to feel bad. I am forever grateful to those friends who put a steady arm around me while I cried or who listened for endless hours while I processed a major life event.

The other friends are those I call when I'm ready to move on. They have no patience for my wallowing in pain or self-pity, but they are wonderfully encouraging when I take the first tentative steps forward. They coach, they cheer, they see possibilities that I cannot yet see.

LET OTHER PEOPLE SUPPORT YOU

Marilynn, who shared her story of recovery in Part One, had been sober in a 12-step program for years and thought her life was finally manageable, when she suddenly was downsized out of a 14-year career *and* lost her life partner to someone else..

"I found myself in a hallway that felt more like a coffin with the lid nailed shut—no light and no air, and filled with grief and despair. I sat on my back porch—cried, spewed in my journal, talked on the phone, shriveled up and withered in spirit and body and refused to accept life. A therapist friend finally shed a glimmer of truth and a definition on my condition: She said I was experiencing a total identity crisis.

"I was too tired, too hurt, too afraid and too weak to re-make myself, and why bother anyway? The hallway appeared endless, and I didn't even care. But my friends cared, so I suited up and showed up one minute at a time because that's what I knew how to do. I needed to feel their love, and they listened to me, hugged me, and they believed that I would pass through (this experience) if I kept breathing and showing up.

"Somewhere deep inside me, I knew I would see the sunlight and feel something besides sadness again. I had to grasp hold of their reassurances and have faith and keep waiting for those damn doorways to appear. I had come so far already. I had no idea when or even if the grief would subside, but I absolutely knew a Power greater than myself was in charge. I knew any rebuilding would not be of my making—I didn't even want to rebuild, nor did I know where to begin. And I sat in that hallway, and I sat in that grief.

"I had to trust the process and believe them when they said 'this too shall pass.'"

What I admire about Marilynn is that she stayed conscious in her pain. She endured emotional upset and loss without seeking escape. She put one foot in front of the other without knowing where it would lead. And she let other people love her through the process. She accepted help, human and divine.

"A full year passed before I felt the shift, and I knew I had crossed a huge threshold somewhere behind me. I had been led by God, expressing as the people I'd allowed into my life and my heart."

Marilynn's shift—and notice, she became aware of it sometime *after* she crossed the threshold—did not restore her life exactly as it had been. Her partner never returned, and Marilynn was single for many years. She never went back to work in a corporate job. Her hallway led somewhere new, as many do.

In the hallway, Marilynn took nearly every step I'm going to suggest in coming chapters.

* She acknowledged her pain but affirmed it would pass.
* She did not judge her feelings as wrong or weak. She just felt them for as long as they lasted.
* She trusted powers greater than her own—human and divine—to uplift and guide her.
* She took responsibility for moving through and out of the hallway, if only by showing up each day.

Marilynn emerged with a much clearer picture of who she is and the purpose of her life. She is pursuing and furthering that even now.

DON'T RUSH TO GET OUT

Regardless of how you think life works in the great cosmic scheme of things, we probably can agree that once you're in a hallway, the only relevant question is not *Why Me?* but *What Now?* One bit of advice from those who have been there: Don't rush to get out.

"I did the best I knew how, and I didn't know very much," John wrote when he shared his story from a lifetime's perspective.

"It happened 40 years ago. My first wife died two days before my 40th birthday. I was a supervisor in life insurance and traveled almost every week. I had two children, ages 9 and 15, and I was in a lot of fear about how I was going to keep my job and yet care for my children.

"I hired ladies to stay with the children, cook for them, etc. while I had to travel, but that just didn't work out. Eventually, I decided to get married again. I wanted a housekeeper, and guess how I treated her! It lasted one year.

"So far, all of my decisions were based on fear. It was surely hell in the hallway.

"My oldest daughter graduated from high school, so I put her up in an apartment. She got a job and enrolled in junior college. I brought my youngest to Dallas with me.

"Eventually, I married again for the same reasons. I had five states to cover, so I traveled a great deal. I did a great deal of damage with my relationship with my younger daughter, trying to give her a good home and trying to hold my marriage together. It took about 20 years to heal that damage.

"We divorced after eight years. It was around this time I discovered (a new spiritual path) and now was learning the principles needed to put my life back together. I spent many years in the hallway of fear and confusion. I was ignorant, confused and stressed all those years. But I am grateful for the experience, for it led me to find and experience the peace, power and love of God."

John, like so many people who have been in the hallway, found spiritual answers to his life questions. He eventually was ordained as a minister and also remarried happily for a final time. But that was years after he made the common mistake of trying to avoid the uncomfortable hallway by racing through the first door he saw.

The hallway is a place of gifts and growth. You can learn from it and make the time count for something, as long as you don't panic and try to flee. You might look back on this experience as a pivotal point in your life's journey. God won't waste your time.

BITS OF WISDOM

* ✴ Most hallways start with the same feelings: surprise, panic, blame and self-pity.
* ✴ You are experiencing grief. Something has been lost, even if you chose the change.
* ✴ No matter what has happened in your life, your thoughts now will create your experience.
* ✴ The work of the hallway is not to fix a specific problem but to meet a spiritual challenge.
* ✴ Friends will hold your hand, then push you forward. Allow their support.
* ✴ Don't run from discomfort too soon. Take time to receive the gifts and growth.

THIS PRAYER IS FOR YOU

Turn within now. Be still and know the divine Presence within you. You are shielded, guided and loved by this Presence, and you are part of it. Immerse yourself in its strength and release any fear.

This may be one of the most important periods of your life. Keep breathing, keep showing up, keep feeling whatever you feel without judgment.

Whatever has gone before, is past. Whatever is next, is yet to come. Let this moment be the place where you dwell. This is where you can realign your heart with Spirit, where you can tap into the well-being of the Universe.

Keep returning to this awareness. Keep breathing.

12 Jerry's Story: Leaning Into Pain

By Jerry Magar

It was a big step for us. Alex and I had been dating a year. In love and exploring where our relationship might take us, we decided to go on a vacation to Yosemite National Park. Our first trip together. For me it wasn't just a vacation. It was a test. How would we travel together? How would we deal with being in each other's presence, uninterrupted, for a week? What might this week foretell of our future together?

With all the gravity placed upon this trip, I was relieved when the stunning beauty of our first morning's hike overshadowed the distraction of the Compatibility Audit running noisily in the background of my mind. We hiked up Nevada and Vernal Falls, sprayed with a mist of rainbows and glitter all the way up, and then out onto a precipice that overlooked the valley. As we reached the summit, we breathed in the beauty and let it fill us. Just at the moment I was thinking to myself: "Cols would love this—she would be screaming with joy, exalting the wonders of God's creation," I heard Alex say, "I wish Cols were here. She would love this."

Cols. Colleen. My closest friend and soul mate. I've always thought that term a bit dramatic, but it is the only way to describe our relationship. From our first meeting eight years prior, there was an immediate and profound connection. To all those who knew us, we were essentially a married couple and, except for the fact that I'm gay and was falling deeply in love with Alex, it made perfect sense. Our lives were intertwined in the most mundane and extraordinary of ways.

As we returned to camp, both exhilarated and exhausted from our morning's hike, I saw the pink "While You Were Out" message taped to our tent. A strange sight in the forest of a national park. As I read the note, my heart quickened. I made the call from a bank of pay phones near the park headquarters. I still remember the strange sound that issued from my throat, a deflating kind of moan and wail all at once, primitive and deep. I remember the concerned, then embarrassed, glances of a group of campers walking by. I remember the burning of my face, the collapse of my knees and the tearing of my gut.

Later, when I learned the exact time of her death, calculating the difference for time zones, I shuddered with the realization that at the same time we were wishing for her presence at the top of a California mountain, Colleen was gasping for her final breath in a doctor's office in Texas.

RUINED

About two hours later, we were on our way to the San Francisco airport to return to Dallas. I wept the entire way, thinking I was ruined. I was convinced I would never recover—too much of me had been torn away. Like a victim of the bear attacks we'd been warned about that morning, hanging by a thread to life, my injury was simply inoperable. I knew I had lost the capacity to experience joy again and wondered how long it would take before Alex would have to make the decision to re-join the living and leave me to my lifetime of mourning.

Three months later, most of the technicalities had been handled. Her room in the apartment she shared was completely cleared out—belongings dispersed, decisions made. The services and memorials were over. Friends no longer called to discuss the tragedy over dinner and too many drinks. It was over. Life was moving on. Except it wasn't, not for me. I had fallen into an endless well of despair and saw neither a glimmer of light from the top nor a glimpse of solid ground below. I was in a freefall of anger and loneliness and pain.

Alex was wonderful during those months—patient beyond measure. He would quietly hug me or hold my hand when he would notice tears flowing at the most random and unprovoked of moments. While I appreciated him for it, I knew that the emptiness that filled me spilled out and into our relationship. And while I loved him, I also knew that it was the love that existed before Colleen had died. I was so dead, so empty inside. There was no way anything new could grow within me.

I had to do something. And I decided that that something would be nothing.

I had a business trip to Cape Cod scheduled. I decided to add another week to the trip and STOP. Stop looking for the doors. The ones that I knew I deserved. The ones that would lead to relief. To life. The ones that would lead to the answers of what's next. I would embrace being in the hallway. For seven days I would disconnect from everyone and everything and simply be. A list of simple rules: No external stimuli. No reading. No TV or movies. No communication with friends or family. No distractions to escape from myself. The point was not about deprivation but about exploration, the internal kind. I brought art supplies and a journal to capture whatever discoveries might be made. And for a week, I sat squarely in the darkened hallway of my life.

... AND BREATHE

Each day started and ended with meditation, something new and difficult to me then. I liked the ritual and routine of it, in the midst of my unstructured days. Days filled with great spaciousness and unpredictability. Days filled with walks, bike rides and long drives through tree-lined roads. I spent one morning in a graveyard, nestled among my new acquaintances, the Hawk family, sketching the stones that marked their spent lives. On another day, I spent the afternoon by a lake, sitting on a bench with a plaque that read: "Dedicated to Michael Welch. Sail on, dreamer." He had died just a couple of years before, at the age of 42. Like Cols, taken too soon.

I sat there imagining the life and death of Michael Welch and the holes that still existed in the hearts of those who loved him.

Other days were filled with painting, drawing, journaling and crying. Hours lying on the hotel bed, sucking in shallow, gasping breaths, my stomach cramping from the repetition of my sobs. Hours wandering through small towns, my heart filled with the weight of her absence. And more journaling. Pages and pages of thoughts captured. Thoughts that made me laugh. Thoughts that made me cry. Thoughts that made me rage. Anger spewed out like wretched vomit. Anger at Cols. Anger at myself. And especially anger at God. There is a great feeling of both freedom and terror that comes with telling the Creator of the Universe that He has supremely fucked up.

In the actual moments of writing, I was filled with both relief and horror. Relief at the luxury of finally expressing in detail the pain that had been welling up inside me. Horror that such things could exist in the depths of my being. The seeds of darkness had taken root and grown deeply in the moist soil of my despair and self-pity. Would it continue to grow and strangle the life out of anything good and pure that remained within me? My conservative religious upbringing reminded me that good people didn't have such thoughts about God. And they sure as hell didn't write them down. There were moments that I was certain any chance of a pleasant afterlife had been dashed by my impetuous blathering.

In the midst of all of this, I would find myself again and again pacing the hallway in which I had been exiled from life. Many times I found myself breathlessly running up and down the blackened corridor, in search of those elusive doors, my desperate fists pounding on the smirking, empty walls. And then it would occur. Silence. An awareness of my awareness. And I would return to the empty floor of that hollow hall, present, still, awake. And breathe. Abandoning the search for escape. And breathe. Embracing fully the crushing pain of the moment. And breathe. Laughing at the absurdity of my humanity. And breathe.

THE POTENTIAL FOR BEAUTY

Piles of sketches and paintings and a bulging journal later, I was home. When asked by friends and family about my "odyssey" (emphasis on the ODD, in their minds), it was hard to respond to the question. Mostly they wanted to know if I had fixed my problem, come to peace with Colleen's death or found what I was looking for.

It was difficult to explain that the experience was not about finding a solution—in fact, part of the process was to have no expectation. The only thing I knew for sure was that I needed to STOP. For only in the stopping was there created a place for starting. Starting to be still. Starting to be present. Starting to hear the Voice inside—the Voice that transcends the static-filled chatter of obsessive thought and is powered instead by the breath of the Divine. And it was here in these moments that I started to learn.

I learned that at times, I still can be swallowed by sadness. And the sadness can remind me of the gift of life rather than the cruelty of death.

I learned there is the potential for finding generosity and beauty in the worst of circumstances, if we are open to seeing it. When a friend learned Colleen had died on Alex's birthday, instead of the usual—"oh, how awful for him"—she smiled and said, "How wonderful. All those years before, on the very day He knew Colleen would leave you, God brought into the world the perfect person to help you through the pain of her loss and to become the enduring love of your life."

I learned, as Rumi says, out beyond all notions of right-doing and wrong-doing, there is indeed a field. And in this field, I've been met with forgiveness and healing. It is a powerful thing to forgive yourself, the dead and the Creator of the Universe.

Finally I've learned that while stopping is crucial, *going* is vital, too, for each helps to define the other. I am learning it is possible to live a life filled both with searching *and* serenity, to be both dynamic and at rest. And it is this life I seek today. A life that honors the terrestrial forces of gravity—of being grounded, rooted, and present; and the celestial forces of lightness—of weightless exploration and expansive possibility. From here, there is no hallway. There are no doors. There is only the profound moment of Now, fully experienced, followed by the infinite spaciousness of what is next.

13 Where Is the Good?

Early in my career as a minister, I walked into a hospital room where a beautiful young woman from my church was being treated for heart problems. She didn't say hello or thanks for visiting. She sat up in bed and said, "Don't tell me I created this."

So I shut my mouth. There's a time and place to consider why events or circumstances have come into in my own life, much less to speculate about someone else's spiritual condition.

But the questions eventually will arise in the hallway: *Why me? Why now? Why this?*

Sometimes the cause is obvious: an elderly parent had been failing for years, a marriage had long been in trouble, an illness or addiction had grown worse, you knew your company would be downsizing. In other words, this difficult time was predictable, which still doesn't mean you were prepared for it. Other hallways are sudden and unexpected; you are thrust into them by events. Even in the midst of change you chose for yourself, such as embarking on a new career or moving cross-country, you might wonder what you could have been thinking when you deliberately closed a door and stepped into the hallway.

Any hallway can feel like hell at times, no matter the circumstances that put you there. And at those times, you're likely to ask some version of: *Why me? Why this?*

Which brings me to the most difficult but also the most empowering lesson of the hallway: You chose it. It's not happening *to* you, it's happening *for* you.

Stay with me through this chapter, please. You might be saying, "Oh sure, I knew that." Or you might want to throw the book across the room. (Or delete it from your e-reader!)

Many people acknowledge that their thoughts and attitudes influence the events of their lives, until something bad happens. Then they disavow any role in it; they claim they can only play the hand life dealt them.

So please consider this slowly and carefully: Each of us chooses every hallway we enter, every time. No matter how much we might appear to be innocent victims or want to believe we had nothing to do with circumstances that seem forced upon us, these experiences have a purpose. Many purposes. Many gifts. Somehow hallways are necessary to our life paths, and we draw these experiences to us.

TRAVELING TOGETHER

That includes the hallways that seem to be brought on by others' crises. I'm thinking of a woman I know whose son was paralyzed in a diving accident. (And as I typed the word *diving*, it came out *divine*. A *divine* accident? What possibilities for good could make it so?)

I know a man whose wife is dying of cancer. I know

a woman whose husband's mental state has made her marriage very lonely. Multiply them by millions. Most of us, at some point, will be in a hallway brought about by the events in someone else's life.

You did not create their circumstances. But if you are involved, then it is bringing gifts and growth for you as well.

For example, I received great learning and gifts from the process of my mother's death. I didn't create her death. She died because she had finished her soul's work on earth for now. She chose, at the deepest level, to complete this human experience and return to the other side.

My soul agreement as her daughter was to participate in her dying process, carry on with my life afterwards and learn whatever was mine to learn from the experience.

Do you see? Somehow events work together for the highest good of all, even with each of us creating our experiences individually.

THE ROLE YOU PLAY

I almost wish I didn't have to suggest that we play a role in creating our hallways. But the cry, "Why is this happening?" is a demand for redeeming value, for purpose and meaning.

Your being in the hallway is not a mistake, and you are not a victim.

This idea is not New Age or woo-woo. Ancient wisdom tells us we are the creators of our experience, and that our thoughts attract people, events and ideas as we need them. This spiritual law has been taught by the masters for thousands of years.

* The Buddha said 2,500 years ago, "All that we are is the result of what we have thought."
* The Hebrew Bible says, "For as he thinketh in his heart, so is he." (Proverbs 23:7 KJV)
* Jesus said, "The measure you give will be the measure you get back." (Luke 6:38 NRSV)

They were not saying we are to *blame* for whatever happens in our lives or that we *wanted* specific events to occur. They were saying we have more creative power than we have imagined, as well as the responsibility to use it as consciously as possible.

Of course you weren't sitting around thinking about a car accident or cancer before it happened. But you might have been living in stress or resistance that kept you out of alignment with well-being. We all do sometimes. You might have shared in our society's general sense of vulnerability, holding the belief that driving is dangerous or bodies inevitably break down.

The most obvious example of our creative power is the placebo effect. Sick people get better when they believe they will. The pill they took wasn't a miracle drug. Their thinking made them well. Medical study after medical study reveals the incredible power of the mind.

People also die when they believe they will. The *nocebo* effect simply means that negative expectations produce negative results.

If you cannot bear to entertain the notion that you played any role whatsoever in creating your hallway or that the experience could bring good to you in any way, come back to this book later. The pain may be too fresh now.

The advantage of seeing yourself as a creator, however, is that it allows you to find meaning in an unexpected or unpleasant experience.

Of course, I've been told I am "blaming the victim" by suggesting we create our experiences. But the concepts of *blame* and *victim* result from having judged an event to be bad and wrong, unfair and undeserved, a senseless tragedy.

I know it can feel that way. But what if we shift the question?

Asking *why me,* or refusing to consider that good might come from pain, leaves you in a state of victimhood. It leads to thinking God is arbitrary and callous, life isn't fair, and bad things happen to good people.

If that's the case, and it's everyone for himself, then why even get out of bed in the morning? Believing this happened *to* you gives you endless justification for bitterness, anger and pain with no responsibility to do anything for yourself.

But what if somehow it happened *for* you? If you chose this experience, consciously or more often unconsciously, then the divine part of you is offering an opportunity for inner work and insight. It's like going back to school before starting a new career—challenging and often not optional. A new level of understanding is required.

Of course it hurts now, but what if this episode leads to a glorious new period of life? What if it is a necessary part of a magnificent manifestation? Life is like a cross-country road trip. Sometimes the scenery is bleak, but it is leading where you want to go, to the destination you truly want at your deepest, most divine level of desire.

HEALING THE MIND

Brenda railed against a diagnosis of breast cancer in her 40s.

"Why was I the one to get his awful disease? I wasn't done with living! Would I make it? I struggled with these questions. I knew that positive thinking was important and that you create your reality. So why, why, why did this happen to me? Why in this day and age when we know as much as we do, why?

"This went on for at least four weeks into chemo. One day I woke up and I knew that if I was going to heal this, I was going to have to take responsibility for creating this. I knew I had to take responsibility for curing this. This didn't mean I would quit chemo and go think myself well; this meant I would start taking responsibility for what I was thinking. Was I really positive? Was I really taking care of myself? Was I really listening to my body and what it was trying to tell me?

"I had to heal myself in my mind and realize I was responsible for me and what I wanted to become. Once I knew this, really knew this and asked God for help, I knew I could walk through this because I could release the outcome and concentrate on just today. That is all I had today. Just today."

Brenda said she developed an appreciation for every moment and compassion for every person. And she got well. Like so many people who traverse the hallway consciously, she said later she wouldn't wish such a difficult experience on anyone else, but she also wouldn't trade the learning and growth she received from it.

Did Brenda create or attract the cancer? Not consciously, but she certainly used the situation for her spiritual growth. An opportunity to develop gratitude and compassion fulfilled her soul's deepest desires.

My personal belief is that each of us comes to earth with a broad outline of lessons we want for our soul's growth. Think of it like a vacation adventure with zip lines and rock climbing. Challenging, sometimes scary, but exhilarating and worthwhile. You go home with an expanded view of yourself, pleased with your courage and accomplishments, or at least with great stories to tell. Such is our time on earth as spiritual beings having a human experience.

How our soul lessons will be achieved through human events may or may not be worked out before we are born. I tend to believe the big events—a lifelong partnership, an early death, a physical disability—are soul contracts to further our growth. This is not predestination. We still draw experiences to us, and we may choose differently as we go. But I suspect we sketched the broad strokes beforehand.

Of course, we are likely to label these experiences bad, wrong, unfair, painful or hellish when we encounter them on earth. That doesn't make them any less useful. The work of the hallway is to shift our thinking from victim to volunteer, from "Why did this happen *to* me," to "Why did this happen *for* me?"

And why did it? Because this hallway is the quickest, most direct route to what you really want. Maybe you want changes in your human life, or you want lessons for your soul. Maybe you actually want to learn how to deal with loss or difficulty. Whatever you are going through is fulfilling your deepest desires for growth and learning.

This is a difficult teaching, and many of us will claim to accept it before we really do. We might continue to kick, scream and resist in the hallway, even while giving lip service to the spiritual opportunities available through pain.

I wish I knew better how our energetic patterns work together with universal laws to create events. Most of us in the hallway had no idea we were choosing a major life change or agreeing to participate with another's. Nearly everyone wants to know why on earth he or she would have chosen this circumstance and what possible soul purpose it could be supporting.

You might or might not receive a definitive answer in this lifetime. But even without it, you will garner gifts and wisdom. You can find meaning for your life—deep, profound meaning—that you could not have received any other way.

HAVE ANOTHER TISSUE, DEAR

Barb said her husband announced after 17 years of marriage that he wasn't happy and wanted out.

"Initially trying to make sense out of something that made absolutely none, I decided straightaway that if this was going to hurt SO deeply, I wanted to learn something from the experience," Barb said.

"As in most divorces, I started out at the lowest of lows, and time dragged so slowly by. All I wanted was to be two years down the road and out of the pain and grief—and out of the hallway!

"After a false start with a really crummy 'have another tissue, dear' counselor, I found a terrific counselor who slipped in little phrases like, 'The Universe wanted you to learn a lesson.' Never really thinking in this way before, this man got my attention."

Now personally, I bristle at the notion that God/the Universe *sends* lessons or *tests* us. It's not the Universe that wanted you to learn a lesson; instead, *you* wanted to learn the lesson, at the highest level of your consciousness. Your own divinity or Higher Self is at work in your human experience.

But I know many people are comforted to believe a supreme being is watching from a distance and protecting them. The events of their lives make sense in terms of "God's will." Others might call it karma that balances our learning experiences over many lifetimes. Still others might be so angry about the hallway—angry at life, at God, at circumstances—that they are bereft of any spiritual awareness.

We each have different theologies and concepts of God or a higher power, including non-belief. My purpose is not to convert you to a particular point of view but to remind you that we have access to power, strength, guidance and hope as we traverse a dark hallway and look for the next door. We will find the door through our own divine leanings, our unerring radar for our highest good.

Barb was willing to do the work of the hallway and let the experience of her divorce further her growth. She eventually gave up anti-depressants, left her divorce support group, sold her house and trained for a triathlon.

"These lessons helped propel me into a new life and appreciate all my blessings and lifted my self-esteem," she said.

DON'T STOP THE REEL

Pain can be an extraordinary teacher, but I do not believe for a minute that we have to experience pain in order to grow. I believe we can learn through joy as well. We draw to us what we need for our soul's growth in the best way available at the time. We attract the conditions necessary to satisfy our deepest intentions. And we don't always know consciously what those intentions are, especially when life is hurting.

We've all walked through hallways where we opened unexpected new doors and eventually walked out into bright sunshine. The firing that led to a much better job. The divorce that led to a much happier relationship or greater freedom. Our deepest desires were fulfilled. An experience was required to get there, and left to your own devices, you probably wouldn't have chosen it. It happened *for* you.

I have a friend who wants to create a line of greeting cards specifically to acknowledge the wonderful outcomes that result from difficult situations and hurtful people. Call this imaginary company Silver Lining Inc.

"Thank you for acting like a jerk," the card might read on the front. Then inside, "If you hadn't left me, I never could have _____" fill in the blank, describing how much better your life is now.

Another friend reminds me often that life is like a

movie on film. Don't stop the reel on any single frame; it might be an ugly or frightening moment in the story. If you don't let the reel keep turning, you'll be stuck in the bad part and never get to the happy ending.

I love the line: *Everything will be okay in the end. If it's not okay, it's not the end.*

This is more than glib reassurance. It is a sign of spiritual maturity to remember that our lives are always in process and that any given moment is propelling us toward greater good. Even the moments that hurt like hell.

Manic Screaming

We should make all spiritual talk
Simple today:

God is trying to sell you something,
But you don't want to buy.

That is what your suffering is:

Your fantastic haggling,
Your manic screaming over the price!

—*Hafiz (tr. Daniel Ladinsky)*

BITS OF WISDOM

* What if this experience is happening *for* you, not *to* you?
* The hallway is not an accident, and you are not a victim.

✳ Even a loved one's circumstances—an illness or job loss—might be bringing gifts for you, too.

✳ Consider that, at the deepest level of your soul, you had a hand in creating this experience.

✳ What you're going through now might become part of a magnificent manifestation later.

✳ This might be a sad or scary scene in your life, but let the movie keep playing.

THIS PRAYER IS FOR YOU

As you close your eyes and breathe, quietly consider that this could be happening for you, an experience born of divine love.

You ask what good there could be? Well, what good have you already seen? The love and support of friends? The chance to reassess your life?

You came to this planet for opportunities to grow your soul in ways you could not accomplish otherwise. What if your soul has brought you to this experience for that very purpose? Can you take responsibility for moving through it with conscious awareness? Can you give up the label that this is "bad?"

If that seems impossible, at least consider that good can come from it. Someday.

Someday all this will be clearer. Let the movie keep playing. In the meantime, know your time is not wasted, and you are deeply loved.

14 So, Where Is God?

When I write and talk about the idea that you are creating your own experience, I often get the question: "Where is God in all this?"

And when I talk to people in pain, they, too, often ask: "Where is God?"

Belief in a divine presence can provide tremendous strength and comfort to those grappling with change. They want to release the weight of the world to stronger shoulders and trust that order will emerge from chaos.

But I'm not advocating a divine rescue. I fear that turning to a big, strong God who is supposed to fix everything carries the risk that you will lose all faith if things don't work out the way you hoped. You set yourself up for disappointment if you pull up a chair in the hallway and do nothing while you wait for God to open the next door.

The God you need is in you. Your own divinity is being called forth. The way you express Spirit in human form will have to be part of the solution.

It might seem to be a contradiction to say you are the creator of your own experience, and yet you can surrender to a power greater than yourself. Both are true.

Yes, you are creating your life, consciously or not. And yes, it is possible to let go and let God.

PEACE NO MATTER WHAT

Consider this story of Lois and her elderly mother, a typical hallway that is no less heartbreaking for being such a common experience.

Lois's mind was spinning with worry and what-ifs while her mother was ill.

"My mother had developed serious medical conditions that resulted in surgeries and lengthy hospital stays. Her condition became so grave that the doctors doubted she would live.

"At the time, I lived 3,000 miles away, was divorced and raising a young daughter and had a full time job. Financial resources were limited, and a round trip plane ticket cost $1,500. Needless to say, however, I flew home to be with my family, expecting the worst.

"Upon arrival at my parents' home, I was told that mother kept saying she wanted to die because she was in constant pain. In the hospital my mother had lapsed back into her childhood and was repeatedly crying for her mother. She didn't recognize my father or any of her children.

"During my daily visits, I would hold her hand and talk to her as though I were her mother, which seemed to calm her. Every day I prayed for God to heal her.

"The days wore on, and I had to think about returning home to my daughter and my job, but I feared that I would arrive home only to find she had passed during my return flight. Filled with guilt about leaving, emotionally and physically exhausted, I prayed silently during the long flight. My emotions ran from anger to pleading with God not to let her die.

"At some point, a calm came over me, and I told God that I released Mother to his care and, whatever the outcome, I would accept she was where she needed to be."

As it turned out, Lois's mother rallied and lived another two years. But Lois was at peace with any result. She prayed, and she surrendered. Both are keys to the work of the hallway.

LETTING GO

If you are in transition, a moment might occur when you stop lingering in the past and also stop projecting into the future, when you release all thoughts of how things ought to be or might turn out, and simply experience the way things are. Without labels, without hope or agenda, you let it be. Whatever is going on, wherever you are, you breathe and let go. You release your resistance and, staying present in that moment, begin to ease your suffering.

That is surrender.

How to let go? Many people pray, but religious beliefs are not necessary to become quiet and feel the flow of well-being through the universe. Some people meditate to find this sense of peace in the present moment. Some hit bottom and simply give up, which creates an opening for the divine.

Angela's daughter was so severely anorexic that her heart was damaged by the age of 14. She spent months in an eating disorders program, her life in danger, with Angela keeping vigil.

"I checked her breathing a dozen times every night and was almost deranged from fear," Angela said.

"One day the nurse therapist instructed me to feed her a slice of cheese pizza for dinner. I felt foolish buying a pizza for this pitiful child, who generally ate grapes, if anything. (At one point, she ate 12 grapes a day.)

"She was wearing a heart monitor, was not allowed to exert herself in any way, and I told her she had to eat a slice of pizza. To say she went crazy on me is an understatement. She ran to the bathroom, locked herself in, and started screaming. I stood in the hallway and was completely engulfed by hopelessness.

"She screamed for at least 15 straight minutes. I slumped to the floor crying, my body slamming against the hallway door, shutting it. I was in a dark hallway that day, literally and spiritually.

"At some point, I told God that I knew I could not control the outcome of this situation. I could not make her eat. I could not make her stop screaming. I could not make her heart work.

"I remember the moment that my grief poured out and emptied, and God poured in. In an instant, my daughter walked out of the bathroom and shoved past me, walking to the kitchen. She ate a piece of pizza. From that day on, she ate a little more each day. It was a miracle."

Angela's daughter went on to graduate from college, marry and now has three children whose grandmother dotes on them.

ACCEPTANCE AT ALL LEVELS

For me, surrender means giving up the stubborn belief that life should be fair or make sense in any given moment.

One of my many flaws as a minister is that I get angry when a congregant receives a serious medical diagnosis. I'm not angry at the sick person, of course, but at life, at disease. It's not fair! All this illness and injury, all these surgeries, all this uncertainty. And cancer, cancer, cancer, cancer! Who will get the bad news next?

I want to wave a wand and make everyone happy again. Which, of course, is not how life works.

We live in paradox, a state in which two things that appear to be opposites are both true. We are indeed creating our experiences or attracting events for specific reasons. At the same time, accepting whatever shows up in our lives is the first step on the spiritual path through the hallway. Accept what has happened, accept the way things are, while also accepting your power and responsibility to design your life from this point forward. Both are true, and both are possible.

No one understands surrender better than alcoholics and addicts whose first step is to admit they are powerless over their disease, that their lives have become unmanageable. Sam wrote his story describing that initial relief:

"I'm seated at a table surrounded by people who love me. They're trying to start me on a journey that begins in this dark hallway where I take my first steps into sober living.

"The first spiritual tool I was handed was

surrender—surrender old ideas, surrender to my own lack of power, surrender to a life of faith rather than fear, surrender to the reality that love is always the answer. It works when all else fails.

"Surrender, I believe today, is one of the most powerful and useful spiritual tools that, when practiced, can lead to a peaceful and serene life. Walking through the hallway, I found a door that opened to an entirely new life, one constructed with a toolkit of spiritual principles such as acceptance, forgiveness, humility, service, willingness, courage and honesty.

"I'm certain to this day that God held my hand through that hallway, because left to my own devices, I would have cut and run. I am as grateful as I know how to be for having walked and been led through that hallway."

Time and again, I have heard stories in which acceptance and surrender were the turning point in the hallway. They didn't necessarily change the circumstances, but they altered the consciousness of those who were suffering. Acceptance and surrender brought about peace of mind.

MELTDOWNS WORK, TOO

Rachel's experience of surrender in difficult and controversial circumstances changed her life forever. She was leaving an unhappy marriage when she had a fling with an old flame. She became pregnant, and the flame vanished.

"So here I was in a tiny apartment, going through a

hellish divorce, pregnant, rejected by the guy I thought I loved, and totally unsure how to proceed—keep the baby or terminate the pregnancy? I really thought my life was over as I knew it. And it was, thank goodness!"

She decided on abortion, "a very difficult decision to make, the right decision at the time yet one that left me in a terrible state of depression."

Then one day, the smallest thing—her garage door wouldn't open—triggered a complete breakdown.

"I literally threw myself on the floor and had a major fit. I was crying and screaming hysterically at God for letting me get into this mess and for not rescuing me before it got this bad. I'm sure the neighbors were ready to call 911.

"Amidst this meltdown, a small, calm voice began to speak to me in my mind. It sounded like my own voice, but it was saying things that I couldn't and wouldn't have said. It certainly got my attention, and I decided it might not be a bad idea to listen.

"The voice gently and soothingly told me to relax and let go. I was to completely surrender and trust that God actually was in charge, and that although things seemed bleak in that moment, in truth, all was in divine order and soon enough, my life would be better than ever.

"I took a really deep breath and surrendered right then and there on the floor. I gave up the fight and in the next moment actually found myself on my knees mouthing a prayer of gratitude for the events of the last three months. Somehow, I was able to reach down deep enough to the kernel of Truth that rested at the bottom of my heart and realize that everything was meant to be for the highest and best expression of my soul's purpose.

"It happened just that fast. One minute I was in hell, kicking and screaming in the hallway, the next minute I was being comforted by Spirit and realizing the real nature of my recent experiences. In that moment, I was transformed and never again felt the angst and depression I had harbored for the past few months. I knew that things would improve, and they did: that healing was imminent, and it was; and that God's guidance through the remainder of the process was assured.

"I have never *not* felt his loving Presence since that day."

Notice the elements of Rachel's story: She listened, she surrendered, she felt surprising gratitude in difficult circumstances, and she affirmed her soul's purpose. Alone on the floor, without the approval of society or support from anyone, Rachel opened herself to a spiritual awakening.

BITS OF WISDOM

* You are the creator of your experience, and at the same time, you may surrender to a higher power.
* Surrender may occur in a quiet prayer or a screaming meltdown.
* Release all thoughts of how things ought to be, and simply experience the now.
* Notice the well-being that surrounds you. Breathe.
* Give up the belief that life should make sense in any given moment.

✻ Listen for the still, small voice that reassures you life will get better.

THIS PRAYER IS FOR YOU

There is a Presence within you now that can heal your broken heart. Let go of any anger or questioning, and be still for just a moment. Feel this Presence surrounding you, permeating your very soul.

This is the divine part of you that can never be hurt or in grief, that is always strong and at peace. Breathe into the depths of your own soul. Release all thoughts to stop the *whirlwind* of *what if* and *what now.*

Deep within you is a peace that passes understanding. You are not facing this alone. Whatever is required of you in coming days, you will be supported and loved by a power stronger than you can imagine.

No matter the difficult moments in your life, the energy of love and power that we call God is with you in every moment.

15 A Time to Forgive

No matter how you got into the hallway . . .

No matter what you think caused it . . .

No matter how much it hurts now . . .

And even if the experience will serve you in the long run . . .

You no doubt have something or someone to forgive. Forgiveness will be crucial to moving through the hallway and finding a new door.

You might have to forgive the person or situation that closed a door in your life. Forgive the spouse who left, the parent who lingered for years with Alzheimer's, the boss who misjudged your abilities, the doctor who missed an early diagnosis.

And don't forget, you will probably have to forgive yourself, too.

The key to forgiveness is to stop insisting on what *ought* to have happened, to stop making up stories about how your life should have been different.

The Greek word for *forgive* means "to untie the knot." Once untangled from the past, you will be free to move forward.

THE OTHER WOMAN

Charlene's marriage came to an abrupt halt when her husband said he was leaving her for another woman, one of Charlene's best friends.

"As couples, the four of us had taken vacations together and even attended the same church. She and I worked for my husband. We were also room mothers together at school. Our youngest sons were best friends. My world as I knew it came crashing down around me.

"While it was not easy for me to wrap my mind around my husband's leaving, it was far more difficult for me to fathom 'the other woman's' betrayal of our friendship. I remember thinking, 'Why didn't someone choose *me*?' I felt broken, abandoned and alone. There were moments of such despair that I wondered if I would ever stop crying and would beg God just to let me close my eyes and not wake up.

"I was angry at God, and I would shake my fist at the sky and scream obscenities into the air. Everywhere I looked I saw 'perfect' families and happy couples. I wanted to get even, I wanted revenge, and I wanted 'them' to hurt as much as I did.

"Then somewhere along the way, in a moment of self-pity and sobbing, a quiet thought came to me: 'If this is how I feel over being betrayed by only two people that I trusted and loved, what must Christ have felt?' I couldn't even begin to imagine a betrayal of that magnitude. While my hell in the hallway didn't disappear overnight, in that thought I had hope that 'this too shall pass.' I knew I would survive and be better for it."

Charlene's story illustrates a primary lesson of the hallway: The pain is in the resistance.

Of course you're going to hurt if a spouse or friend abandons you, or a loved one dies, or your life is up-ended in some way. But the worst suffering is the result of thinking, *Things should be different, this shouldn't be happening, it isn't fair, what if,* and *why.* Every thought feels like a stab wound until you are able to accept, forgive and release.

Forgiving the dead can be especially complicated. A drug overdose. A suicide. The parent who left a mountain of debt. The spouse who died just as you were looking forward to retirement. You loved them dearly and miss them, yes. But it's possible at the same time to be furious at the way they died or the moment they chose to leave the planet. Furious at what happened to them. Even more furious at what happened to you.

Deep breath.

The pain is in the resistance, in believing things *should* have been different or *ought* not to have happened. Within those judgments lies your suffering.

Did you ever think of that? I was surprised to learn years ago that I only had to forgive the people I had judged to be wrong in the first place. It wasn't someone else's actions but the animosity burning in *my* heart that required me to forgive. I created these feelings of blame, judgment and ill will, and I had the power to release them.

Consider the destruction of a relationship, for example, whether it's romantic, with friends or relatives, or at work. For me, the worst part is afterwards, combing through every hurt, slight or humiliation, every lie or misunderstanding—and letting go of them, one by one. Ultimately, I have had to forgive people for not being who I thought they were, or who I wanted and needed them to be.

In those situations, I also have had to forgive myself. For trusting. For loving. For making the choices I made. Sometimes for being blind and stupid. For projecting my fantasies and shadows onto someone else.

You see how long a forgiveness list can grow? How in the world can you release it all?

Not even the experts who study forgiveness know exactly how it comes about or can pinpoint the exact moment it occurs. But if you become willing, one day you will realize you have forgiven and will know you have been blessed.

"IT WAS NOT OKAY FOR ME TO HATE"

"At some point I was able to forgive the man who raped me," wrote Robin. "Then it took a long time to accept that forgiving him was all right. Many therapists and friends told me it was okay to hate him. After a while, I just stopped trying to explain it. It was not okay for me to live with that hate.

"He is in jail serving three life sentences, and there are at least 15 of us who have DNA evidence he was the person who raped us. I'm thankful for that and for the police and people who worked to catch him. His last victim that we know of was a 12-year-old girl who knew his son and recognized his voice. I can't imagine the courage it took for her to identify him. I never knew her name, but I'm grateful for her every day. He belongs in jail and should stay there. But I can't even imagine how damaged a soul must be, to be that violent to so many people he never even met. I feel sorry for him.

"I'm also grateful to learn that I have this amazing heart, will and life-force (don't know what else to call it) that are like steel. It still shocks me that that person lives inside me.

"One day I just realized I had forgiven him. I knew for sure that it was over when I delivered teddy bears to the rape crisis center—they use them for therapy with children—and there was no energy left around being there and what happened.

"It will always be with me, but it's not there in a painful way anymore. I always had faith it would happen eventually; it's just still surprising."

Robin later finished a master's degree in social work and now serves at a hospital as a victim advocate and crisis counselor for domestic violence and rape.

"I started working here 20 years and two weeks after I was one of those women in the ER," she said. "It took a while, but I am really happy about being here."

That is grace, when you know you have been healed. You have forgiven. You are free.

ANGER: RIGHT AND RIGHTEOUS

The only thing worse than having to forgive something truly awful is not to forgive at all. Refusing to forgive is like drinking poison and expecting the other person to die, or holding onto a hot coal, intending to throw it at someone else. Who gets burned?

Clinging to old feelings about an unhappy past is self-harm. It traps the anger, hurt and blame that eat you from the inside.

Don't beat yourself up for feeling those emotions at times in your life. Just make sure to clear them out eventually.

Here's something useful to know: Anger is a part of grief. Grief, as we've said, is inevitable in the hallway. Something has been lost, a door has closed, even a door you wanted to close. So don't be surprised to find yourself inexplicably irritable, and maybe explosive, in the midst of a major change.

This is why families tear into each other over funeral arrangements or fight over a tiny inheritance. A table. A ring. A silver tea set. This is why stories of illness or death so often include disproportionate outrage about a doctor, minister, relative or friend who said the wrong thing at a sensitive time. The anger of grief is why lawsuits can drag on for years.

Admit it: Anger and blame can feel good. They are energizing. Righteous indignation! Telling everyone about this affront! Holding on for dear life to the knowledge you've been wronged!

And maybe you have been terribly wronged. But does drinking pain's poison make you feel better?

Forgiveness does not condone the act. Notice in Robin's story, she will never believe it was okay to be raped. It will always hold significance in her life. But in letting go of hatred, she is no longer controlled by a sick man or a single incident.

FORGIVING YOURSELF, PART AND PARCEL

The most difficult act of forgiveness, of course, is self-forgiveness. Again with the *shoulds* and *oughts*. *I shouldn't have been there. I shouldn't have trusted. I ought to have known. I ought to have succeeded. I ought to be a better person.*

Every act of forgiveness boils down to self-forgiveness.

I didn't believe that when I first heard it. Sometimes other people are just wrong, I argued. I might forgive them, but the bad acts were theirs, not mine. Weren't they?

Except that I was involved. I participated in some way, if only by being in the wrong place at the wrong time. More often, my very deliberate actions, decisions and choices put me into situations or relationships that ended up hurting me. And at the metaphysical level, I believe I attracted it.

For all those reasons, I have to forgive myself.

Sometimes we even have to forgive specific parts of ourselves. A body that got sick. A brain that went blank on test day. A tendency to overeat or snap at the children or lie to avoid conflict. We've all got our stuff. We all have parts of ourselves to forgive.

So, what does forgiveness have to with the hallway? Just this: You are moving through a period of transition and, in time, you will open the door to a new part of your life. You don't want to drag all this baggage with you. You don't want to carry the hurtful people and events of the past into your new day, with ugly memories clanking like a ball and chain.

TWO PATHS TO FORGIVENESS

There are two kinds of forgiveness.

Traditional forgiveness: You believe someone else has wronged you, but you don't want to hold feelings of ill will for the rest of your life. You let go of the hatred or disappointment or anger.

Metaphysical forgiveness: You are able to see that what happened was perfect for your soul's growth. You learned from the experience or worked through issues that had been with you since childhood (or perhaps a past life). You might never label the event good, but you see its gifts.

It might help to know which kind of forgiveness you are working toward.

May I suggest further reading? Of course, there are many good books about forgiveness, but if you are interested in four steps to traditional forgiveness, try *The Book of Forgiving* by Desmond Tutu and his daughter Mpho Tutu (HarperOne, 2015). And to understand the perfection in any situation, read the classic *Radical Forgiveness* by Colin Tipping (Sounds True, new edition 2009).

You don't have to choose between these two types of forgiveness. You can experience both. You might let go of negative feelings first, then see the gifts you received. Or you might see some of the gifts even before you release the upset.

Forgiveness lets you lay your burden down. Leave the past in the past. Travel light through the next door. Emerge from the hallway clean and renewed, even nourished.

How, exactly? I know no better method of forgiveness than simply to become willing to forgive. When the person or event comes to mind, breathe, pray and release. Ask to see it differently. Ask to see the good. Reclaim your life from obsession with others. Do this as many times as it takes, for as long as it takes.

One day you will look back without emotion, without a knot in your stomach, feeling neutral and at peace. You might even wonder what all the fuss was about. And you will see clearly the gifts you received.

> The sages have taught you to love your enemies and forgive those who persecute you, but what they forgot to tell you is that you are powerless to achieve this on your own. You can cultivate a loving heart through prayer and fearless self-inquiry, small acts of kindness, and more radical acts of social justice. You can turn toward your pain and say yes to your life, but you need the God of Love to meet you halfway. You cannot forgive without grace, and grace is not something you can demand. You can only sweep out the chamber of your soul and be ready to receive it when it comes.
>
> And when it does, there is not a doubt in your mind that you have been blessed. No effort of your own could have yielded this lightness of being.
> —Mirabai Starr, *God of Love*

BITS OF WISDOM

* ✳ Forgiveness is crucial to leaving the hallway and opening the next door.
* ✳ Pain is caused by believing that your life should be different than it is right now.
* ✳ You only have to forgive the things or people you have judged to be wrong in the first place.
* ✳ You might have to forgive others for the way they lived or died or just for being who they are.
* ✳ You might have to forgive yourself for choices you made, actions you took, even feelings you felt.
* ✳ Ask to see it differently. Ask to see the good.
* ✳ Forgiveness is both miracle and grace. Your role is to be willing to forgive.
* ✳ One day, the anger and pain—the emotional charge, the energy—will have dissolved. You will be free.

THIS PRAYER IS FOR YOU

Let go, dear one. Release and let go of this awful pain inside you. Can you at least become willing to forgive? Yes, someone in the past was wrong. But you deserve better than to let that person run your life now.

Gently let go of the blame for yourself, too. Whatever you did or didn't do was your best at the time. You deserve better than to beat yourself up forever.

The events of the past might never be something you understand. But they are over. And in time, you might see their perfection, if you are willing. In the meantime, I AM right here with you, within you.

You are entering a new phase of your life. Let yourself be guided away from any judgment, blame or self-righteous indignation. Move forward to a fresh and clear new day, into the divine light that welcomes you.

16 Power of Prayer

Giles spent 55 days in the hospital, unconscious, on a respirator. He didn't know until much later how many people had been praying for him. But he told his minister he wasn't surprised, and he wrote about his experience:

"Even though I was unconscious, I have a dim recollection of some force at work within me. I can give no real names to this force or the sensations it produced, other than to describe it as if I were being struck with some sort of balls or pellets that were forcing me upwards, like a bottle-nosed dolphin might nudge a drowning man toward the surface of the water and to the safety of the shore. Like that man in the sea, I was drowning in the infections that were assailing my lungs, and it was only the prayers of the people who interceded on my behalf that brought me back to the shore of this life."

Nearly everyone with a hallway story mentions prayer, whether prayers for themselves, their prayers *for* others or the prayers they received *from* others. Most of us can't explain exactly what prayer is or why it works, but humans instinctively seek a conscious connection with a greater power.

If anyone says, "Let me know what I can do to help" while you are in the hallway, ask for prayer. It is the most effective action anyone can take on your behalf, regardless of what you or they believe about God, even if you believe nothing at all. Prayer is focused thought that moves the creative energy of the Universe.

Ask them to affirm your highest good without worrying about the specifics of what happens next in your life. Let their loving thoughts buoy you.

And as you pray for others, please remember, love is not the same as worry. Worry blankets those we love with our fear; we are imagining the worst for them. Love holds a vision for the best, in whatever form it takes.

THREE FACES OF GOD

One of the common criticisms of religion is that people create God in their own image, projecting human qualities onto a deity, insisting that God loves and hates the same people they do.

The critics are probably right. How could it be otherwise?

Our limited human brains cannot comprehend the magnificence of All That Is. Therefore, our image of God is whatever we need a higher power to be, called by whatever name we choose—Father, Lord, Buddha, Dharma, Chi, Spirit, Life, Love.

Most of us have only a glimmer of understanding of the divine. But ideally, our ideas about God deepen and our consciousness expands over a lifetime.

The way you pray will depend on how you think about the divine—what it is, how it works and its relationship to human beings—at any given point in your life.

I found help in sorting out my understanding of God from Ken Wilber, an American philosopher, who speaks about three basic ways the divine presence is described in the world's religions. When I first heard it, I recognized all three but realized I had jumbled them together when I tried to talk about God, confusing myself and probably others.

Wilber calls this the Three Faces of God, the primary ways humans perceive the divine. I'm sharing it here because it might bring you clarity in the hallway, especially if you aren't sure how to pray.

✳ First Person (I)—God within, the divine essence of every human being, the soul or Higher Self that creates and provides exactly what you need for this lifetime

✳ Second Person (You)—God in relationship, the God of traditional prayers, a personal God who knows what is going on in your life and responds with love, forgiveness, comfort and guidance

✳ Third Person (It)—God transcendent, All That Is, the Ground of Being, the Universe, principle, law, creation

Once you recognize these three facets of God, you will begin to see them in varieties of prayer.

Let's start with Second Person because it is the common definition of prayer, and it is the only description of God many of us were taught.

Prayer in Second Person addresses God as something outside and beyond us, yet it is a personal God we can talk to. Typical Second Person prayers might begin with "Dear God" or "Our Father," a deity with a name.

This aspect of the divine could also be a relationship with angels, saints or higher beings in whatever way you imagine them. It is prayer as dialogue. You are communicating with something.

Jewish philosopher Martin Buber called it the *I and Thou* relationship, making ourselves available to God even if we cannot truly understand what God is.

Prayer in First Person was a mystery to me when I first began to learn that God is within me. Was I praying to myself then? I didn't know where to aim my prayers.

First Person prayer is probably best described as affirmations, declaring the Truth of your being. It calls upon the divine within to strengthen and uplift you. It reminds you of your divine essence.

I am a beautiful, dynamic child of God.

I live in a universe of abundance.

I have everything I need to carry out my life's purpose.

Affirmations don't make something true; they remind you what already is true, how the Universe works and who you really are as a spiritual being. First Person prayer shifts your consciousness from the level of personality to the divine, so you can create your life from a higher level.

Prayer in Third Person celebrates the awe and mystery of God. If you say "Wow" when you see a beautiful sunset, that alone is a Third Person prayer. These prayers acknowledge the magnificence of creation and the transcendence of the Source.

They also invoke spiritual law, the universal principles we live by. Anytime you are working with the Law of Attraction, for example, or deliberately creating your life with your thoughts, you are working with God in Third Person. (To read more about spiritual laws, my earlier book is entitled *The Five Principles: A Guide to Practical Spirituality.*)

Gratitude fits in this category, too. Some of the most spontaneous, heartfelt prayers are simply, "Thank you." You don't have to address God with a name, you don't have to get on your knees, you don't have to understand the workings of spiritual principles. Just say thank you.

No single face of God is better or more accurate than the other two. They are like tools in a drawer, to be used as needed. Each represents a different way to think about the divine—and to pray—at different times.

MY VIEW OF PRAYER

Spiritual beliefs are deeply personal, and prayer varies accordingly. I can only describe what has worked for me and how I understand the power of prayer and faith.

For me, the relationship between God and human beings is one of co-creation. This won't surprise you, since I have been insisting throughout this book that we are the creators of our experience and our thoughts have creative power. We are divine beings expressing God on the earth. (This is a First Person concept of God.)

"The Father and I are one," Jesus said. (John 10:30 NRSV)

Father was the term Jesus used to describe the divine Presence at work in and through us. *Father* was an idea his followers could relate to in terms of love, protection, guidance and provision. Sadly, *Father* was later interpreted to mean an old man in the sky, a male deity watching and judging our behavior.

I am not a pawn or puppet of a supreme being who wants to control my life. I believe Spirit works in me, through me and as me for good on the earth. The universe has been arranged so that I can create my experiences through the power of my thoughts and feelings.

That's why I say being in or out of the hallway is my own creation. Not that I necessarily planned for it, asked for it or wanted it consciously, but somehow I drew it to me as a way to address my deepest desires for learning and growth in this lifetime.

What does this mean for prayer?

Some people worry they are edging God out if they claim their own divinity or see themselves as creators. But remember, it's co-creation, you and God. Saying you play a role in creating your life does not mean you are doing all the work by yourself. God is right there, within you and all around you.

You've seen in these stories how frequently people talk about their reliance on the divine, how they were able to surrender and pray even amid tears. The same support is available to you. You are never alone and never separate from the Source. You can call upon that Presence anytime, using any type of prayer.

But even though you may lean on God, something else is also true. As you have read in these stories, many people say they could not begin to move out of the hallway until they took responsibility for being there. They consciously began to create the lives they wanted.

So it's both/and. You act, and so does God. You and the Father are one.

CHANGING VIEWS

A trip through the hallway is often an incentive to update and deepen your understanding of God and prayer.

John L. was a conservative Christian who adjusted his views over the years. He said his hallway experiences used to be simpler when he believed God was running the show entirely. Now John believes he has his own role to play but, like nearly everyone, he struggles with the paradox of creation and surrender.

"Growing up a fundamentalist, I *knew* that the way I looked at things was the same as God looked at things. So not only was I unshakeable in my own convictions, but I was equally unshakeable that anyone who believed differently was wrong," John wrote.

"Such strong conviction does give great comfort in the hallway. No matter what the situation, I knew that God was in control, that Romans 8:28 was operating (" . . . *all things work together for good for those who love God* . . ." NRSV), and that the entire situation, taken as a whole, was specifically designed to bless me. With such core beliefs, I had no need to know why I might be in a hallway. I drew comfort from my assurance that it all had a purpose."

Later, after a period of doubt and change, he found a church that taught the divinity of all people and the creative power of thought. John still believes he is carrying out his soul's purpose but no longer assumes every situation is "God's will" being forced upon him for his own good. Understanding that he volunteered for this human experience and its growth opportunities is empowering for him, but a little scary.

"In the past, there was nothing that I considered to be my responsibility to move me forward," John said. "Now I believe the responsibility is totally mine."

Whether you imagine that you are cooperating with God's plan for your life, carrying out your soul's purpose or balancing the karma of past lives, all things *do* work together for good in the hallway if you allow it. The benefit is from consciously participating in the work of the hallway, taking responsibility for your experience and lessons while there, trusting that whatever needs to happen will happen, then finally moving toward the next door.

DANGEROUS PRAYERS

I want to offer you several prayers to use in the hallway, but I have to warn you, these are dangerous prayers. Dangerous because they work and because they can invite unexpected, sometimes shocking developments into your life.

The first is this: *Reveal what needs to be revealed, and heal what needs to be healed.*

This means you might discover things about yourself you didn't know, don't like or hadn't remembered. They are coming up now to be healed. You are strong enough, and the healing is necessary for your journey forward.

Many people in the hallway have been stripped of outer trappings. You might feel as if there's nothing left but you and God, eye to eye. This is an excellent time to explore who you are, how you got here and what you want next.

You might find some ugly parts of yourself that had been hiding in shadow are now revealed. You might also find some forgotten nuggets of gold deep within. *Reveal what needs to be revealed.* Let whatever you need to know for this phase of your life be revealed.

And if you find qualities, habits or beliefs that no longer serve you or are holding you back, they may be healed and released.

For example, someone in the hallway after a divorce might pray *Reveal what needs to be revealed* and might be shown his or her part in the split, or some longtime behaviors that have always caused trouble, or some negative beliefs about relationships that guarantee failure. Once those have been dragged into the light, they can be released or redeemed.

Again, it's co-creation. You'll do some of this work yourself and depend on grace for the rest. How do you know which is which? Take every action you can think of while holding the thought: *Heal what needs to be healed.* You will be showered with ideas, new avenues for action and people who can help you. You will make amazing progress, even if some of your work is arduous.

The second prayer is: *Lead me where you need me, and speak to me in ways I cannot possibly misunderstand.*

See what I mean by dangerous prayers? Are you truly willing to receive a clear message?

The *you* in this prayer—"lead me where *you* need me"—might be God, your Higher Self or Inner Being, the Universe, life. At this point, what matters is your willingness to hear the guidance. You are listening for direction that will lead you to a place of purpose for yourself and service to others.

Notice that these prayers are not about throwing up your hands and demanding that God take over. They are collaborations with God. You are asking for work to do; you are offering to put feet on your prayers. Co-creation.

In addition, these prayers ask to find meaning in painful circumstances, to open your eyes to what you might not be seeing. That's a prayer in itself: *How can I see this differently?* It never fails to shift my perspective.

Or simply pray: *Show me the good.* Then watch for good to show up.

I have a friend who says her prayers through the years have boiled down to one line: *I hold all possibilities.*

We live in a field of infinite possibilities; we are immersed in an ocean of abundance. Anything can happen; our highest good is available. Any situation can turn out in a wonderful way—we've all seen it. We don't have to know what will transpire or how. We can hold all possibilities.

Remember Ed, who was facing a second round of chemo? I later prayed with him in the hospital, and he offered his own prayer along with mine. He began, "What a joy it is to be here."

By *here*, he meant in oneness with God, in a universe where all things are possible. He was so sick that day, he couldn't stand up. But he said, *What a joy it is to be here,* aware of the divine presence that is always within.

Could you do that? To pray *what a joy it is to be here,* no matter the circumstances? That might be the ultimate spiritual courage.

One more thing: Whatever you ask in prayer, give

thanks in advance. Saying thank you for what you already have received is good manners. Saying thank you in advance is faith. It affirms your belief in an abundant, friendly universe.

Living from gratitude opens you to receive. Your good awaits you behind the next door, as you begin to move out of the hallway.

BITS OF WISDOM

* Every human being is a part of God and has an unbreakable connection with the divine.
* Prayer is focused thought that moves energy.
* If anyone offers to help you in the hallway, ask for prayer.
* Love is not the same as worry. And prayer is not worry.
* The way you think about God determines how you will pray, and there is no right or wrong way.
* Prayer is collaboration with God to design your life together.

THIS PRAYER IS FOR YOU

Pray: *Reveal what needs to be revealed, and heal what needs to be healed.*

Pray: *Lead me where you need me, and speak to me in ways I cannot possibly misunderstand.*

Pray: *How can I see this differently? Show me the good.*

Pray: *I hold all possibilities.*

Pray: *What a joy it is to be here.*

And let the prayers of others heal you, soothe you and lift you up. They are manifestations of God's love for you.

17 Lisa's and Jan's Stories: The Healing Hallway

LISA: MAKING THE DECISION

Lisa was a trim Dallas executive whose sudden ill health appeared to make her a victim of fate. She didn't know the term "hallway" at the time, but her beliefs and choices exactly tracked a successful journey through transition.

* ✳ She first believed the experience was something forced on her.
* ✳ She resisted it.
* ✳ Then she accepted reality.
* ✳ She even saw how she had brought it about.
* ✳ She took responsibility for dealing with it.
* ✳ She used spiritual tools, including imagination, to create what she wanted behind the next door.
* ✳ She moved on.

For years, Lisa had performed important jobs within a prestigious global corporation, but this promotion was the high point: international marketing manager. She was literally in charge of the world.

This new job carried a steep learning curve. Lisa immersed herself in the details, keeping track of foreign offices, traveling and trying to do everything right, to please everyone.

Every night after work, she complained to her husband, "I can't assimilate all of this. I'm so confused."

During the day, as data poured in from every direction, she kept telling herself, "I'm gonna throw up."

Her body broke down during an international business trip, less than four months into the new job. She was sick, exhausted, couldn't sleep, couldn't make decisions, and she had severe stomach problems. By the time she dragged herself back to the United States, her body had stopped digesting food altogether.

She entered a long hallway of uncertainty and disease. Her kneecaps came out of their sockets, and she couldn't walk without a cane. She suffered from anxiety and depression. She couldn't digest medicine. And she spent hours on the Internet, reading about illness.

"The more I focused on what was wrong with me, and I researched and looked into it, the worse it got. Or other symptoms would come up. The doctor hated to see me coming.

"It wasn't until five or six months into it that I said, You know what? This isn't working."

She had been given the option to leave her job altogether and live permanently on disability. Somehow that prospect shook her awake.

"I realized I was defining myself as an illness, that I was becoming these illnesses, and it wasn't really who I was," she said. "I didn't want to be sick, and I didn't want to be unhappy. I wanted to be joyful."

Once she set her intention to get well, her experience began to change. Lisa found a new doctor who not only diagnosed her ailments accurately and offered some helpful medicines, but who agreed that the illness and the healing were created from within.

"I just knew that I had not taken time to be who I was," Lisa says. "I was so worried about being perfect for everyone else. I knew the answers were inside. I'd known for a long time but I wanted to ignore it. I wanted to look outside. I wanted to blame other people, or (trust) doctors and let others control my destiny."

The new doctor wouldn't play that old game. She told Lisa: "You have to make the decision to be well."

Lisa said, "I started going to church, started reading, started listening, started having fun again. I quit focusing on what was wrong with me and started looking at what I wanted to be and what I wanted to do. My intention was to get through it and move on and be whole and healthy."

In retrospect, she was amazed at the power of her thoughts and words to create an illness.

"I remember the self-talk—'I'm gonna throw up'—and guess what? I did! I would get so much thrown at me that I remember thinking, 'There's no way I can assimilate all this.' And I'll be damned if I couldn't digest anything."

She had been recovering at home for a year, living on a reduced salary, when her employer began calling, enticing her to come back. Courting her. What kind of job would she like?

Having realized her power to create her life, Lisa playfully decided to create the perfect job. She met with the bosses and described exactly what she would like to do, without mentioning any specific position.

Together, they devised the job of her dreams, and she went happily back to work, feeling productive and making sure she balanced her life to keep from being overwhelmed.

"It wasn't until I accepted the belief that I was in total control, and that I had the power to turn this around, that I did."

JAN: BLESS IT AND RELEASE IT

Jan woke up from a colonoscopy with a doctor standing over her.

"This isn't good," he said.

"Okay.

"No, this really isn't good."

"Okay," Jan said again. "So what are we going to do?"

Many years later, Jan told me, "It was in that moment that I knew all of those classes and all of that spiritual training, all the things I'd been working on all my life, really worked. I had no fear. I wasn't looking forward to what was going to happen, but I went, *Wow, I'm not afraid!* I was actually saying that to myself while I was still lying on the bed in the lab."

Jan agreed to three months of radiation and chemotherapy before surgery. The operation took just two hours instead of the forecast 5 ½ hours, and the malignant tumor already had shrunk from 5.2 to 1.2 centimeters.

The doctor bragged to the staff about his brilliance.

They told Jan on a follow-up visit, "Dr. S. has been talking all week about the surgery he did. It was the best, most perfect surgery he's ever done!"

Jan has other ideas about the source of her healing.

Just days after the diagnosis, she had spoken to her minister, who said, "Don't fight this. Anything you fight, fights back. Love it, bless it and let it go."

Another minister had called to pray with her every day. He was beside her hospital bed on the morning of surgery to pray with Jan and her son, the doctor and nurses.

And Jan had put into practice all the lessons of her lifelong spiritual exploration.

"My faith increased, so even if it didn't turn out like I thought it would, it was going to be okay."

Shortly before the surgery, Jan felt she received a message from the divine: "Love is the key to life."

All the lessons in her illness and recovery seemed to be about love.

One day in the grocery store, when Jan was exhausted from treatments, dragging herself through the aisles, "This lady from nowhere came up to me and said, 'I want you to know you are being so blessed, that God is taking care of you.' It was exactly what I needed at exactly the right time."

Her coworkers took on Jan's health as a project, making sure she ate even when she didn't feel like it, bringing her whatever salty or sweet food might tempt her.

Instead of losing the average 60 pounds expected during her course of treatment, Jan lost just 18 pounds. Her friends wouldn't let her stop eating!

"I was able to feel the love that was around me, and

that changed my life. It warms your heart. I learned to pass that on to other people, to let people know they're important, to let people know you notice the things they do, that they do make a difference."

But what stuck in her mind most were the words of her minister: *Love it, bless it and let it go.*

"It applies to everything! There are so many opportunities I've had to use that," she said.

"I lived my life differently. I was much more open to love. The little things don't make such a difference anymore. Everybody has different stresses and things that set them off, and I'm not free from that. But overall, it was a total shift in my life.

"I'm not nearly as controlling about things; I let things go. I learned how precious life is. That's why they call it a gift.

"I also learned to put up shields. There are situations that I don't want to be a part of, and I don't take that on. There's something you can learn from every situation, and sometimes it's RUN."

Best of all, Jan has been able to share with others the lesson of *Love it, bless it and let it go.*

I asked what else she might tell someone who has received a scary diagnosis, and she offered these ideas:

* Fear blocks healing, so several times a day, remember just to breathe. Inhale the healing light that penetrates every cell in your body, and exhale anything unlike the nature of perfect health.
* Don't become your diagnosis. You are not your disease. Instead of saying "I have X," say, "I have received a diagnosis of X." Encourage your

friends and family to do the same. Don't claim the illness as part of who you are.

* Don't overdose on information. Poring over test results or going online to look up more about your diagnosis and symptoms can fill you with fear. Stay focused on your healing.

* Read something that uplifts you spiritually every morning and evening.

* Spend time creating affirmations, listen to music, watch something funny or hang around people who are fun and will keep you encouraged.

* Jan also was able to keep working throughout her treatment and recommends it, if possible. She stayed busy and useful and soaked up her coworkers' support.

* Healing happens in many ways, and not only for the person who is sick. Those around you might experience emotional healings. You can be sure there is healing in every situation.

Jan remains especially grateful to the minister who told her to *love it, bless it and release it.*

Years later, when the same minister was diagnosed with cancer himself, Jan urged him to remember his own words of wisdom: *Love it, bless it and release it.* At this writing, they both are cancer free.

18 Volunteers, Not Victims

Even though it may be deep and unconscious, each of us calls forth exactly what we need to satisfy our life's purposes. Other people are dutifully playing their roles, and they, too, are learning and growing.

So you can let go of "why" you're in the hallway—you know why. This was the only way to achieve what you really wanted at a soul level.

The hallway has no victims, only volunteers. You are in the hallway for the same reason you came to earth in human form—for the experience. You wanted the gifts and lessons, joys and sorrows it brings. You knew the human journey was an opportunity to advance your soul.

The prayer, *Reveal what needs to be revealed and heal what needs to be healed,* opens you to the spiritual work of the hallway. To pray, *Lead me where you need me, and speak to me in ways I cannot possibly misunderstand,* indicates a willingness to find the next door.

Not everyone likes to imagine that Earth is a school or life's challenges are for learning. Some people hated school. Some are exhausted from what they've already learned, or they believe they're doing fine without need for further growth, thank you very much.

We all feel that way sometimes. In seminary, we used

to refer to life's challenges as AFGO: Another F***ing Growth Opportunity.

But think of it this way, perhaps: Our souls were living in a state of pure bliss, in divine light, love and understanding, when we decided to send a part of ourselves to Earth. We booked an excursion and donned the human spacesuit because we wanted to practice divine love in an environment that is truly difficult, to learn how to love and be loved at depth, whatever it takes. It might require forgiveness, it might involve physical disruptions, and it was bound to include collisions with the billions of other souls taking this trip at the same time. But we came for the experience, for the spiritual practice, even for the drama.

And we came for the joy. For the beautiful days, the spectacular sunsets, the mountains and flowers, the laughter, the music and art and dance that express the Spirit within us. And certainly we came for the other people, for the exhilaration of love, even with all its pain and confusion.

Before we took human form, we knew that as divine beings we would always have access to the One Mind and to the unfathomable love of which we are a part, even while on this crowded and sometimes lonely planet.

We knew that simply by moving through time and space as human beings with a limited view of events, we would find ourselves in transition repeatedly. We would constantly be changing. Such is the process of human life. We are forever closing and opening doors and moving through hallways.

If only we could remember our life's purpose and the choices we made before we came! If only we could see that we are drawing to us exactly what we need for this journey, and that we are guided with every step.

Instead, it's easy to feel like a victim, when every appearance indicates you had nothing to do with your life's difficult circumstances. Stuff just happened. Your body gave out, or your money ran out. Someone hurt you or left you or got in your way.

Nearly all of our major life events involve other people, and we cannot easily wrap our human brains around the idea that each of us is creating with our thoughts, attracting what we need and receiving our highest good. All of us, at the same time. We are not causing events in others' lives, nor they in ours. We are participating in each other's soul choices.

If God is all there is, then every event or circumstance is immersed in divine love. Those we label bad, and those we label good. We learn and grow from both pain and joy, from both difficulty and success, from health and sickness, wealth and poverty. And someday, when we are in some other form, we will know its perfection.

ENTWINED HALLWAYS

It's not unusual to find yourself in a hallway because of someone you love. A child is seriously ill, your spouse can't find a new job or your parent is dying. You are taking a journey together from different perspectives.

Any legal action, court case, criminal charge or lawsuit can become an agonizing period of uncertainty, throwing many people into a hallway together. Doors creak as they open and close, and sometimes jailhouse bars slam shut.

When I spoke to Janet Conner, she was waiting for her 24-year-old son to be released from prison, which she hoped would end a series of legal hallways they had been through together.

Over a period of four years, Gerald Koch had been called twice to testify before grand juries in New York. He lived those years with the knowledge hanging over him that if he refused to answer the federal prosecutor's questions, he would most likely go to jail for contempt of court, much like a reporter who refuses to divulge sources.

That's exactly what happened. Jerry took the Fifth rather than name his friends who were political dissidents or student protestors, including some in Occupy Wall Street, and a very angry judge threw him in jail. He was never charged with a crime. Jerry's mother considered him a political prisoner of the United States.

Now, given that Janet is a spiritual author who writes books about how to access the divine voice within, and who shares an array of spiritual rituals and practices with her students, I wondered how she was handling this ordeal.

"The first 60 days (after Jerry went to jail) were a complete fog," she said. "My spiritual practices went out the window; they just dissolved. These incredible things that have held me, loved me, supported me—I couldn't do it. I was numb."

She slipped into the most comforting place she knew, St. Michael's Shrine, a tiny Greek Orthodox chapel near her home in Florida, and she wrote. And wrote. Because that's how she connects with her inner voice. (Her first book was titled *Writing Down Your Soul*.)

Sitting in the quiet chapel with pen and paper, she implored the divine, " 'You have to help me! How do I pray? How do I pray for my son?' I wrote, 'How would a mystic pray?'

"Then immediately my hand wrote what I call the Perfect Prayer. From the second those words arrived, I knew this is it, this is all I have to pray."

The divine in me, through me, and as me
blesses my precious son Jerry,
honors his soul's divinely appointed mission
and showers him with grace.

Janet has shared the Perfect Prayer widely. You may use it for anyone you love, she says. Just fill in the name.

Janet prayed in the morning and evening at an altar she created for Jerry in her living room, then went about her busy life. She thought, " 'I've blessed him, I've honored him, I've showered him with grace. Now I can go eat breakfast.' It does free me so I'm not quite such a wreck."

Rather than focus on Jerry as a victim of an unjust system, Janet chose to believe this episode was necessary to his life's purpose, his "divinely appointed mission."

"He is here for something holy. It's part of his evolution. I don't want him in prison, he doesn't want to be in prison, but I have to accept there's divine order all the time or none of the time. It has to be okay on some holy, divine level."

Eight months went by with Jerry waiting in a cell and his mother waiting for news. Hour after hour, day after day, neither of them knew what to expect. Janet prayed and enlisted friends around the world to pray, showering love and light onto the formidable Metropolitan Correctional Center in Manhattan.

Then one day, without explanation, guards transported Jerry to the courthouse, unlocked his handcuffs and told him he was free.

Janet's words again: *I have to believe there is divine order all the time or none of the time.*

Even if you simply cannot believe we create our experiences or have anything to do with what happens in our lives, I hope you believe that good and gifts can come from any situation. Those gifts may not be the reason something happened, but they do manifest if we are open to receive. We can choose our attitudes and reactions to life events. And that, too, is the work of the hallway.

NOTES FROM THE HALLWAY

Listen to enough people talk about the hallway, and tips begin to emerge for maximizing the time you are there.

This transition can be a period of recovery and preparation, they say, to gather reserves or marshal forces. It is best used for spiritual reconciliation and renewal that equips you to find the next door and walk into a new way of being.

My friend Laura suggests that leaving the hallway might not really be possible, because we're always on our way to something else. But being out of *hell* is possible.

I have talked to people about the hallway for years,

spoken about it and taught classes on it. I have interviewed people who were in and out of hallways and have solicited their stories in writing.

What follows is loving guidance for your journey, compiled with good wishes from others who have been through the hallway:

* **Don't skip the grieving.** A door has closed and something has been lost. Grief takes as long as it takes. Lean into it, as in Jerry's story. Remember you are probably surrounded by people who would be honored to love you through this experience. Ask them for help. If you don't believe you have such people in your life, ask anyway. The divine touches us most often through each other.

* **Accept where you are.** It's a hallway. It's a transition. Some segment of your life has ended, changed or been overturned, and the next segment may not be clear at all. Resistance turns pain into suffering. Let this be a time of acceptance and surrender, which includes acknowledging your deepest, even ugliest feelings.

* **Take responsibility for being here, even if you don't yet know the purpose.** Every significant hallway brings major gifts if you allow it. My belief is that my soul attracted or at least agreed to the circumstances for my own growth and learning. But even if you insist you are just a random victim of fate, growth and learning are still possible if you open yourself to them.

* **Pray.** If you believe in any sort of higher power—deep within you, surrounding you or watching from a distance—open yourself to its guidance and wisdom. If you have no belief in a divine presence, at least set aside quiet time each day to journal, walk or just breathe. Clear your mind and align with the life force.

* **Become willing to forgive.** Resentment is an anchor, holding you back from the next door. Pray to see the person or situation differently, to release the negative energy that eats you from the inside. Free yourself.

* **Don't buy into other people's experiences.** It doesn't matter whether 99 percent of people with the same diagnosis die within a year. It doesn't matter whether 60 percent of second marriages end in divorce. It doesn't matter that your friend's cousin went bankrupt trying to follow his bliss. Those are other people's experiences. They are the creators of their lives, and you are the creator of yours.

* **Don't get stuck asking for guidance.** Ask other people for help, yes. Pray, certainly. But don't spend your life in the lotus position, continually asking for divine guidance without listening for answers. Become quiet, and open your mind and heart to your inner wisdom. Deep within, you know what to do.

* Imagine one of those flashing signs in a highway construction zone that reads: EXPECT DELAYS. The timing of your recovery and movement forward may be perfect, but I guarantee there

will be days when you are convinced this hallway has no end, no light and no new doors. Even after delving deeply into your spiritual work and reaping as much enlightenment as you can, more fortitude still might be required to open the next door. Hang in there. In hindsight, you might be astonished how quickly a new phase of your life took shape. You might be amazed how happy you became after the hallway seemed so dismal. The timing will be an exact match to your willingness to receive your good. More about this in Part Three.

✳ **Stay in the present moment.** Most of the hell we experience in the hallway is the result of regrets or resentment about the past and fears about the future. How are you doing in this moment, right here, right now? Breathing? You might be in pain, physically or emotionally, but is it bearable for now? The present moment is the only place you can find peace.

BITS OF WISDOM

✳ You are experiencing exactly what you need in order to satisfy your soul's purposes for this lifetime.

✳ Even if you don't believe you created your experience, believe that good and gifts can come from any circumstance.

✳ As humans, we always have access to the One Mind and the unfathomable love of the divine.

* Take responsibility for where you are, even if you don't yet know the purpose.
* Grieve, then accept where you are. Pray, then forgive. Ask for help, human and divine. Stay present.
* Milk every experience for all the spiritual growth and understanding it is worth.

THIS PRAYER IS FOR YOU

Take a deep breath. Feel the good, even if you can't see it or name it yet. If good seems impossible, feel the love. You are not alone here. Many, many souls have been in this hallway, and their divine energy supports and guides you.

What if it's true that everything happening in your life is part of your own plan and has a purpose? What if it really is all a part of God, designed for your highest good and growth?

How long this journey lasts, and where it takes you, will suit you uniquely. Stay present. Keep breathing. Let go of past and future.

Let this be a time of rest, renewal and recovery. This is your preparation to open the next door.

Part Three

Opening the Door

*One day you will feel your heart's healing.
One day you will look up instead of down.
One day you will sleep more deeply. One
day you will breathe more slowly. One
day you'll know more laughter than tears.
One day faith will sustain. One day hope
will return. One day love will beckon.
One day you will know . . .*

*And on that day, probably when you least
expect it, you will see it: the door before
you. And you will be ready. You will step
forward, reach out, turn the knob, and step
right through. Into the light. Into the open.
Into the new. Head held high, shoulders
back, radiating the glory that is you when
fully alive, awake, aware. With a tender
and ferocious heart that is raw, but strong.*
—Ronna Detrick

*Look, I have set before you an open door, which
no one is able to shut.* (Rev. 3:8 NRSV)

19 The Threshold

It's time to open a door and walk out of the hallway.

At last! But how?

How exactly do you end this "hell," this period of reflection and recovery, and start to live your life anew?

Here's what I know for sure: Consciousness shifts first.

By that I mean, your amalgamation of thoughts, feelings, beliefs, attitudes, hopes and expectations—conscious and unconscious—rises to a new level, expands into new awareness.

The breakthrough manifests differently for each person. You might not notice a change until one day, you hear yourself laughing for the first time in months. One day, you realize you're looking forward to an upcoming event. One day, you peer down the dark hallway and see a glimmer of light.

For a few, this shift feels like emerging dramatically into sunlight or turning onto a new street. Ahhhhhh. You know you are out of the hallway, even if you have no evidence yet.

For most, however, this new awareness flickers on and off. On a chart, it would look like an EKG, up and down, some days hopeful, some days back in despair. But at least now, more and more moments are spiking above the flat line.

To be sure, nothing in your outer circumstances might have changed yet. Leaving the hallway does not mean you have found a new job or married again. You still might be caring for a special needs child or a dying parent. You might not have a clue what you want next for your life. But you're spending at least a little time looking forward instead of back to what could have been.

You've stayed conscious through the pain of the hallway. Now stay conscious as you find the next door.

BUT FIRST, DO YOU REALLY WANT OUT?

Yea, though I walk through the valley of the shadow of death, I do not pitch my tent there.

Are you sure you really want out of the hallway? It would have been a silly question early on, but now that you've lived in the hallway for a while, opening a new door might seem daunting.

Don't let this section depress you. Leaving the hallway is quite possible. Just be aware of what might hold you there.

Ken is smart, talented, and delightful, one of those guys who is always on the verge of success. He tells everyone his ship is about to come in, a door is about to open. But somehow, it never quite works out.

"I've never really tried to get out of the hallway," he said. "The hallway is sort of my comfort zone. It's not that I'm afraid to try one door or another—I have many times. But I've never gotten used to the glare outside. I'm uncomfortable in it."

Some people never make it out of the hallway. Doors don't seem to open for them. Opportunity doesn't knock. They appear to be victims of circumstance.

"No one's hiring."

"The prognosis isn't good."

"I have nothing left."

Becoming discouraged in the hallway is not unusual or to be condemned. Everyone in the midst of change worries how things will turn out, wonders whether life will ever seem normal again or whether their best days are behind them.

Life may not seem worth living.

After her husband died, Judith lamented that she wished she had died with him. She was not actively considering suicide. She just couldn't understand why she was still on the planet or what she had to look forward to. She was vibrant and healthy and miserable.

"If I had known this would be so debilitating, I would have gone with him. That very day. I would have said, 'You're going? Take me with you.'"

In extreme cases, people do die in the hallway.

You might have known a few people who lost a job or marriage or who got sick or had some kind of setback and never seemed to recover. Knocked down, some cannot get back up. They might simply drift, they might sink into addictions or they might neglect an illness until they die, all while insisting they just can't get a break.

More often, people die by inches in the hallway, not moving forward, growing accustomed to darkness and no longer reaching for a new door. The hallway can become a way of life, even a comfortable one. You might build a nest there, install carpet and a fireplace, and resent the draft if a door opens for you.

DOES THIS SOUND FAMILIAR?

Why wouldn't you want to leave the hallway? See whether any of these common reasons sound like something you might say or think:

The hallway is comfortable, familiar, predictable. Not knowing has become my new normal. Waiting is just what I do. One of these days, I'll get around to taking action, or some serendipitous event will show me what's next. But for now, what's on TV? Where's that bag of chips?

I've been getting lots of sympathy. My hallway has been filled with loving, supportive people who shared my pain and comforted me with their solicitous attention or even tangible gifts. If I get better, they'll leave me. Alone.

I'd feel guilty if I left the hallway. Moving on feels like betrayal. "What am I going to do if I get to the end of that hallway and I forget about him?" Judith worried almost a year after her husband's death.

I don't know what I want. Or I have so many ideas, I can't decide. And every option scares me! I'm afraid of failure and afraid of success. After being thrust into the hallway, I'm acutely aware that life is unpredictable with no guarantees. I'm afraid of risk.

Who would I be without my story? I've focused so long on the door that closed, I've told the story so many times, I've obsessed so passionately about everything that happened and everything that changed in my life, it defines who I am now. Pain, anger, and blame fill my days and fuel my energy.

I once met a woman over dinner who curled her lip when I described the hallway concept as a means of handling transition. "Don't talk to me about that," she said with a shudder. "My son just died."

It turned out her 38-year-old son had died of cancer four years earlier. Granted, life is never the same after the death of a child, but she was determined to keep the pain fresh and to live in the immediacy of her loss. She wouldn't even discuss leaving the hallway.

Maybe such a reaction is understandable. You might never be able to restore the past as you knew it. A loved one who died isn't coming back and can't be replaced. A divorce is a permanent change. Your health might never be as good as it once was.

So what ends the hallway in those circumstances? Where is the door?

* Peace of mind.
* Knowing you'll be all right, whatever happens.
* Taking responsibility for your life from this point forward.
* Setting an intention to be the person you wish to be.
* Taking a step, moving your feet, beginning to act.

Here in Part Three of the book, you will read more stories of those who found new doors to open. But first, doors opened within them. They couldn't change their outer circumstances until they changed their way of thinking. Consciousness shifts first.

One more thing, as you begin to leave the hallway . . .

Once you feel a little better, you might be embarrassed by some of your recent behavior. In my hallway experiences, I know sometimes I have spewed anger or self-pity, or I enjoyed playing the victim and soaking up sympathy. When you were thrust into a hallway, you might have taken a deep dive into unconsciousness, reacting purely from ego for a while.

Don't beat yourself up about it. We all get mired in events sometimes, and we rant and wallow until finally we're sick of ourselves. Once you become aware of it, you are already moving out of it.

Remember we're not here to transcend the human experience. We came precisely to experience it. Look around and you'll notice nearly everyone's time on earth includes some pain and drama that they might not handle gracefully. Live and learn. That's the point.

THE FIRST STEPS OUT

When I first started talking about the hallway years ago, I could describe in detail how you end up there, and I could suggest valuable work to be done. But getting out? I thought you just had to wait for God to spring open a door.

A few years later, I latched onto the Law of Attraction and said leaving the hallway was entirely up to you. You are the creator of your experience.

Have you ever seen the very early Mickey Mouse

cartoon where Mickey runs to the end of a hallway, hits a blank wall, then pulls a crayon out of his pocket and draws a doorway to run through? Create a doorway like that, I said!

I still believe the Law of Attraction—the universal spiritual principle that our thoughts have creative power—is in effect no matter how it has been trivialized. I'll write more about it in the next chapter.

But I have finally come to see that getting out of the hallway is not God's job or your job but a joint effort, a co-creation, which takes place entirely within you. The hallway ends first in consciousness. You'll probably feel it before you see it.

Zettie did. She was running a business and rearing two girls as a single mother when her parents both became ill, 200 miles away. She made trips back and forth, juggling life so relentlessly that she ended up in intensive care with a serious respiratory infection.

After eight days, she was sent home with a rented breathing machine and was advised to buy her own. She would probably need it the rest of her life to compensate for the damage to her lungs, she was told.

"I felt as though all doors were closing, and I was in that dark hall. I went through the *why me . . . this isn't fair . . . I am so scared . . .* and anger at being in this situation."

During this already dark time in her life, her father died.

"Daddy had always told us, 'You make your own heaven and hell right here on earth by what you think and say and do.' One night I had a dream-like visit from Daddy, and he said, 'Now darling, you are going to be okay. You just need to get your thinking straightened out.' It was so real!"

So Zettie set about changing her thoughts.

"I started each morning with prayer and meditation and asking God for guidance. I visualized each breath coming in with the healing power of God within, and the outgoing breath was releasing the disease.

"Each night my prayer was thanking God for His guidance, protection and healing. I blessed the condition for the lessons I needed to learn. I blessed the doctors for their God-given talent and knowledge. I blessed the medicine I needed to take for its healing power, and I even blessed the breathing machine, which I had so resented."

Four months later, she returned the breathing machine. She didn't need it anymore.

"The door that God opened after the abyss of the hallway was the door of my mind, my attitude and the conviction that this could be changed with God's help."

Read that last sentence again.

Zettie left the hallway in consciousness first, before she saw any evidence of physical healing. She took responsibility for getting out of her own hell, just like Brenda from Chapter 12, who began to recover from breast cancer when she took responsibility for creating it and curing it.

They both worked in concert with the divine.

They also appreciated everything they could think of. "Appreciating that the morning came and I was alive," Brenda remembered. "Appreciating the flowers that bloomed. Appreciating that I felt good enough for that day to get to the couch. Appreciating the people who wanted to help me. Appreciating my family. Appreciating all of the little things that made up my life."

Both returned to their natural state of health.

MAKING THE SHIFT

So what is this shift in consciousness, and how do we make it happen?

I asked my Hell in the Hallway students to list what it takes to leave the hallway, and they agreed the first step is to think about it differently.

Acknowledge you are in the hallway, they said. Presumably you have reached a place of acceptance as you worked through Part 2, but some of us have to face reality over and over again. Life has changed. What is happening right here, in the present moment?

Let go of anxiety and frustration, panic and judgment. Again, this might have to be done over and over.

Be brave, they said.

Trust your light will shine and show you the way.

Cultivate patience. The hallway takes as long as it takes.

Live with gratitude. "It's hard to remain stuck and sad when you are grateful," one said.

Open up and allow vulnerability.

Remember you have come through other hallways.

Remember this is happening *for* you.

"Choose powerful over pitiful," Julie said. This hallway is the breakdown before the breakthrough.

"I learned to trust the hallway," Colleen said. "It's where my soul can grow."

BITS OF WISDOM

* It is possible to become too comfortable in the hallway or to feel guilty for leaving. Be willing to rewrite your story.
* Before any change or breakthrough, consciousness shifts first. You might feel it before you see it.
* We are here to experience life, not transcend it.
* You make your own heaven or hell here on earth by what you think, say and do.
* Appreciate everything around you. Appreciate being alive.

THIS PRAYER IS FOR YOU

Close your eyes and breathe deeply. Can you see a glimmer of light at the end of the hallway? Are you looking forward more often now, planning your future or at least acknowledging you have a future? Are you willing to open the next door?

You can let go of the past without losing your memories or your love for the people who were there. You can let go of the way you used to live without losing who you were and are. Your soul is still expressing God *as you*, even if your surroundings have changed.

You are being shown the way. Trust the door will open when you touch it. Trust the light is on the other side.

You stand at the threshold.

20 Design Your Life

At last you know your time in the hallway is coming to an end. You might feel you have been drifting in the hallway for years. Or you might feel forced by circumstances to open another door as soon as you can.

As you look ahead to the rest of your life, or at least to the next step, there's only one important question: *What do you want?*

You get to choose.

What will you create behind the next door? Will you live the next chapter of your life by design or default?

The awareness that our thoughts have creative power, that whatever we focus on will show up in our lives, is an ancient spiritual teaching. That's how we attract love, money or opportunities. The Universe reflects our thoughts to us.

In the hallway, pain pushes you until a vision pulls you. You've been propelled through the spiritual work of the hallway by your desire to feel better. You have already released any notion that you are a victim. You have long since realized your hallway experience is happening *for* you.

Now you may decide what's next.

Napoleon Hill, whose 1937 book *Think and Grow*

Rich introduced earlier generations to what is popularly called the Law of Attraction, explained there are two kinds of imagination.

* ✳ **Synthetic imagination** is rearranging what is already familiar. You take what you know and tweak it or rearrange it to create a new picture. It makes the life you have a little better.
* ✳ **Creative imagination** is open at the top for new input. It leaves room for divine inspiration and the unknown. It's the future you never could have imagined, with results beyond your wildest dreams.

Designing your life really is not a difficult process that requires metaphysical expertise. It comes naturally. Haven't you already been thinking about what you want next? For that matter, haven't you been dreaming since childhood of what might be possible for your life? Desire is an evolutionary driver. It keeps us reaching for the stars.

DESIRE IS GOOD

The word desire has fallen out of favor because desires are so often labeled selfish or worldly.

But consider: Desire is God speaking directly to you. If you want to know where God is leading your life, study your deepest longings.

Let's explore this for a minute:

When I first heard the idea that thoughts have creative

power, I was worried. My thoughts seemed so . . . random. Often negative. And fearful.

When I heard I was the creator of my own experience, I wasn't sure I wanted the responsibility. Wouldn't I create the wrong things? Weren't my desires selfish?

I had the idea that whatever God wanted for me would be something I definitely did not want. That's why I resisted surrendering. The only way to control my life was *not* to ask for divine guidance.

I gradually began to understand the concept of co-creation with God. Even before I acknowledged my own essence is divine, I could envision a working partnership with a higher power.

But I was rocked on my heels when I read Emilie Cady, the New Thought author of *Lessons in Truth*, who wrote in 1904: "Desire in the heart is always God tapping at the door of your consciousness."

Imagine! Desire is communication from God, offering a gift, saying: "Wouldn't you like this?"

Cady said we would not desire a thing if it were not available to us. Edwene Gaines, a spiritual prosperity teacher, says desire "is a coming attraction in your life."

Of course this doesn't mean you will indulge every passing whim. Look beneath the surface. What is the true longing? What is the feeling you desire?

Whatever we think we *want* is because of how we hope it will make us *feel*.

We long for wholeness. We'll get it wherever we can, and we often go awry, trying to use lovers or alcohol or money to fill that God-shaped hole inside. Suffering is not the result of desire but of our misguided efforts to avoid pain and find pleasure.

Our deepest desire is for divine connection, which we can receive in many ways besides prayer or meditation. Laughing with friends, playing with children, good food, good music, a life-changing book all are experiences of God. Life is full of joy, if we pay attention.

THE PARADOX AGAIN

I'm quite aware that in this chapter, I'm saying you can create the life you want, while in an earlier chapter, I wrote at length about surrendering to what is and letting yourself be guided into a new phase of life.

It's both/and.

You get to make up whatever you want for your life. And you also will attune to a higher consciousness to ask what's next. It's a paradox, when two things that appear to be opposites are both true. You create your life at the same time you receive divine guidance.

I think most people lean naturally toward one or the other, and there's no perfect ratio of conscious creation to dependence on the divine. Both are crucial, and both are available. Once you begin to grasp your oneness with the divine, your own divinity, there's really no difference.

So, with the understanding that surrender is still going on, let me suggest three ways to take the bull by the horns and design the life you want. Use any or all of these, in any order.

1. **Create the Conditions**

The Buddha said when conditions are sufficient, there is manifestation. In other words, designing your life is like tending a garden. With the right timing and healthy soil, with the proper doses of sunlight and rain, you will reap all the flowers or vegetables you planted.

A garden is an excellent example of conscious co-creation. It works like this:

You don't control the seasons, but you decide when to put seeds in the ground. You didn't create the earth, but you can add enrichment to the soil. You don't make the sun shine, but you decide how much light the plants will need and locate them accordingly. You can't make it rain, but you can use a garden hose or watering can to help nature along.

In the same way, you create the conditions for whatever you want to manifest in your life. The seeds you plant are your intentions or desires; they are kernels of your vision for the future. Tending the garden is a daily process of keeping the conditions healthy by consciously aligning with the divine (prayer, meditation, reading, singing, being in nature), appreciating whatever shows up and taking action as needed.

You started creating the conditions while still in the hallway, when you removed rocks and weeds and tilled the soil. Now you continue the work by planting healthy seeds for what's behind the next door.

Janet Conner, who spoke in Chapter 18 about her son's imprisonment, offers a rich 30-day process for creating the right conditions for an abundant life. In her book, *The Lotus and the Lily*, she says not even to bother envisioning what you want. Just "put your undivided attention on your connection with the vibrant presence of the Divine within, and your life will change."

Or as Jesus said, "Strive first for the kingdom of God."

He insisted that if you pay attention to your spiritual development first and foremost, then everything else will fall into place. (It's in Matthew, Chapter 6, if you want to read the whole passage in context. It's part of the Sermon on the Mount.)

Your spiritual consciousness creates the conditions for whatever shows up in your life. Tending, tilling and nourishing your inner state of being prepares you for the blessings of the Universe, just as a garden thrives on sunshine and rain.

2. Go for the Feeling

One of the stumbling blocks to envisioning the future is that so many of us don't know what we want. We just want to feel better.

Actually, knowing how you want to *feel* is an excellent way to design your life. You don't have to know what it will look like. You don't need a sweeping vision or detailed list. You'll recognize success by the way it feels.

So how do you want to feel?

That may not be an easy question. Many people can't get in touch with how they feel. Others know how they feel right now but can't imagine feeling any different. In their minds, this moment, this condition will last forever, whether it feels good or not.

So you might want to start simply, one day at a time. Set an intention before you get out of bed. How do you want to feel today?

Today I will feel joy.
Today I will feel grateful.
Today I will feel lovable.
Today I will feel attractive.

Think about the actions you might take today to bring about those feelings. Simple things.

* If you want to feel attractive, dress up a little.
* If you want to feel grateful, make a gratitude list. Or go outside and express your appreciation to the world you live in.
* Make a list of three things to do today that will help you feel the way you want to feel. Just remember, this cannot depend on anyone else's behavior. You are only in control of you.
* You don't even have to take action. Just set an intention for the feeling you want, then watch what shows up. Your thoughts are magnets, remember? You will attract people, ideas and situations to match your intention.

Decide on the desired feelings, then pay attention to the messages coming from your life—conversations with people, books that leap off the shelf into your path, song lyrics that stick in your head. Pay attention to dreams. Pay attention to opportunities for change or action. Stay present, and take any step you can toward your intended feeling.

After some practice, you might want to settle on the top three or four feelings you would like to have and affirm them every day.

For example, *I intend to feel happy, creative, productive and inspired.*

Or, *I am peaceful, loving and self-assured.*

Stick with your list for a while and see whether your

intended feelings begin to show up more dramatically. Pay attention, and keep saying yes to your desires.

(A lovely book that elaborates on the creative power of feelings is *The Desire Map* by Danielle LaPorte, Sounds True 2014.)

3. Write a Vision

This is such an old trick of manifestation that I wouldn't mention it, except that it works. The primary benefit of writing a vision for your life, besides that it's fun, is your own clarity. What *would* you prefer next? If you could have anything, what would be behind the next door?

Remember to write in present tense, as if it's already here. I was taught to start this way: *I'm so happy and grateful now that* . . .Write as if it has already happened. Go for broke. The Universe has no limits on what it will provide for you. The mere power of your thoughts will begin to attract it.

Be sure your vision includes the four pillars of your life: health, relationships, vocation and money. What do you want in each area, one year or three years from now?

If I were writing a vision for my work a year from now, it would be something like this: *I am so happy and grateful now that* Hell in the Hallway, Light at the Door *has been published! It has been well-received, and I love hearing from people who have found it useful in their lives.*

Then I might elaborate on the wonder of all that has happened. Write as if it's already done.

It's quite possible that your life after the hallway will

never be the same as it was before. But you can envision your future self as happy and grateful that you are at peace with the changes, or that you are comfortable with a new way of living, or that amazing new people have shown up to support you.

OH, THE PLACES YOU'LL GO!

Our playful Universe often puts a twist on its gifts, doesn't it? You get what you wanted, but in ways you never imagined and couldn't have made up!

One of my students said she decided to see the blank canvas of her future as a field of possibilities, rather than emptiness. *How* our visions and desires come about is none of our business; it's not our job. We just choose what we want and let the rest fall into place. It will happen; it's spiritual law.

As you remain open to seeing your good delivered in any way possible, you might be steered in unexpected directions. Moving on doesn't always mean moving away from your hallway experience. Sometimes the hallway event becomes the foundation for your new life.

The most obvious examples are social movements that grew out of personal tragedies. Laws have been changed, advocacy groups established, scholarships and endowments funded. You might find yourself lobbying Congress or counseling others who are experiencing what you went through.

Part of what happens in the hallway is an evolution of desire. You might not end up *doing* what you thought you would, but the *feelings* will be what you desired.

For example, if you want to feel fulfilled, it might come through a job, or it might come instead through a relationship. Feeling self-confident might show up first intellectually and later physically. Keep setting the intentions for how you want to feel, and you might be surprised at the variety of ways a certain feeling is evoked in you.

Spend time with your hopes and dreams. Talk to them. View them without judgment or attachment. The hallway may be life's conversation with you about your greatness.

* Create the conditions by staying in touch with your inner wisdom, your divine or Higher Self.
* Choose how you want to feel.
* Write a specific vision for the life you desire.
* And through it all, pay attention to what shows up—people, events and ideas. Once you are open, the Universe will shower you with opportunities. Like rain on a garden.

My Brilliant Image

One day the sun admitted,

I am just a shadow.
I wish I could show you
The Infinite Incandescence

That has cast my brilliant image!

I wish I could show you,
When you are lonely or in darkness,

The Astonishing Light

Of your own Being!

—*Hafiz (tr. Daniel Ladinsky)*

BITS OF WISDOM

* When you're ready to move on with your life, the only important question is: *What do you want?*
* Engage your imagination. Desire drives humanity to be more and do more. How do you want to feel?
* Put your attention on the presence of the divine within.
* Leaving the hallway is co-creation with the divine. You tend to the seeds and soil, God grows the garden.
* Stay alert. Take any step that leads in the direction of your intention.
* Be open to the good that shows up in unexpected ways. You will recognize it by how it *feels*.

THIS PRAYER IS FOR YOU

Close your eyes and smile. This is the fun part. Start using your imagination to design the life you want.

It won't be the life you used to have and maybe not the one you expected. But starting where you are now, you are free to design your future from this point.

Know that the divine in you is calling forth opportunities, events and people to match your deepest desires. Ask yourself what you really, truly want. Better yet, determine how you want to *feel*, and let life provide the means.

Celebrate the desires you are feeling. They are the activity of the divine in you, God reminding you what is possible for your life. Desire heralds opportunity. Let your desires flow.

21 Go Ahead, Ask for Help

Now that you have some idea what you desire behind the next door, you might want to ask for help in opening it. Human help and divine help.

Let's talk about human help first.

Asking for human help is a little dicey. You might already have been given a raft of advice while you were in the hallway. Depending on your circumstances, you might have been told to develop a hobby or start dating again or adopt a baby. Each well-meaning suggestion was offered with the certainty that it would solve all your problems.

Did you occasionally notice some of the people trying to help you seemed to be tapping their feet, waiting for you to hurry up and feel better? "What? You're still grieving?"

Now that you're ready to move on from the hallway, however, you can ask for their help because it might actually help.

The more clearly you can state what you want next, the better others will understand how to help you. Step up and say, *I'm ready to* _____. And share your desires.

You might be surprised at the network you have, who they know or what tidbit of information leads you to exactly the right place. (*"Lead me where you need me..."*) Even if friends and family can't provide direct resources, they can cheer you on. And what a joy for them to have that opportunity, after all the worry and sympathy they've had for you in the hallway.

They have been singing your song until you could remember the lyrics. You do them great honor by asking for help now. Nearly every leaving-the-hallway story I've heard includes the support of those near and dear.

If you don't already have a spiritual community, the hallway is a good time to find one. Of course, you can be spiritual all by yourself. You can pray and meditate, read and study, create your own rituals and develop your own brand of mysticism.

But it's a little like growing your own food. Admirable, but tremendous effort. Wouldn't it be easier once in a while to drop by the grocery store to pick up a few things? To benefit from the work already done by others?

That's what a spiritual community offers, whether it's a church, a 12-step group or a Buddhist *sangha*. Others on the human journey are sharing their experience, strength and hope as they follow a spiritual path already traveled by millions, who have left books, prayers and signposts to guide you.

Besides, people who regularly attend some kind of spiritual service live a few years longer. It's healthy.

Although leaving the hallway is ultimately an inside job, you don't have to be alone while you do the work. Even if others can't possibly understand how you feel or what you've been through, they can love you and hold a vision of your happiness. Ask them for help.

Human help and divine help are essentially—meaning in their essence, their core—the same thing.

WHEN GOD SEEMS LOST

Maria found help through her friends when she couldn't bear to contemplate God.

She once thought she had created the perfect life in partnership with a beautiful woman and her little boy. Together, they were the family Maria never thought she would have. They would grow old together and dance at the boy's wedding.

Then after 7 ½ years, the woman told Maria she was done.

"I lost God, and I lost my mind," Maria wrote to me.

"My definition of who I was and what I was here to be was smashed in an instant. Unable to pray, unable to even consider God, I walked around like a ghost. I couldn't stop crying, I couldn't eat, I couldn't sleep. I couldn't go to church—(church) was one of the first places we connected those years ago, and the church held too many dashed dreams. We had attended as a family.

"I couldn't believe this was happening. I felt as if I truly was coming out of my skin. This trauma was very physical as well as emotional.

"Buffeted by friends who let me crawl up on their couch for hours (days, weeks, months) and just lie there, I began to walk down the hallway. But I didn't want any of those damn doors or windows that might open up to me. My life was perfect, and now it was over.

"I contemplated suicide and even sat in the garage a

couple of times with the car running. I had two beloved dogs, though, and they would be alone.

"Now when I remember that time and what it felt like, I cry that I was so hopeless. I see the self-pity, and I'm grateful that whatever relationship I had with God was enough to have my wonderful friends grace my life. They kept telling me the truth—the real truth. They absolutely loved me. God showed up through them."

FIELDING OTHERS' OPINIONS

God does show up through those who love us, but with their kindnesses often come their opinions. They just can't help themselves. I think I've discovered a way to make their opinions useful.

When I left journalism to go to seminary, I braced myself for hoots of laughter in the newsroom. It never happened. Only two people thought I had lost my mind: my mother, as I mentioned earlier, and my therapist. Both based their objections on money. Ministers, they were sure, lived in poverty.

As it turned out, I made more money as senior minister in a big church than I ever had as a reporter. But no one chooses either profession to get rich.

In hindsight, I realized the objectors were mirroring my own qualms, the ones I didn't want to speak aloud. They did me a favor by forcing me to look at the financial fallout from my decision. To answer them, I had to be sure *myself* that I wouldn't let fears about money guide my life.

Remember, nothing is in your experience unless it

is a match to your consciousness. If you are surrounded by people objecting to your plans and predicting failure, they are reflecting something in you. See them as agents of the Universe, assigned to bring you clarity.

It's just as likely, however, that objections, fears and qualms will be shouted in your own familiar voice. This is the voice of the Inner Critic, the one that says you'll never get out of the hallway, you've already taken too long, you're a weakling and a spiritual failure and a fraud. And everyone else knows it!

Do you have that voice within?

Standing in a new doorway, the harangue can become especially loud. "There won't be enough money!" "People will think I'm crazy!" "This problem can never be resolved." You can stall for years at the threshold, defending all your reasons for not stepping forward.

Those inner objections and criticisms are the voice of fear, and it is trying to protect you, to keep you from taking on more than you can handle, to keep you from being hurt. Out of love, it does not want you to fail. Fear has kept our species alive, telling us to run from tigers.

But how do we know whether the voice that says *stop, wait, be careful* is coming from fear or from good common sense?

The best answer I've heard is from Rhonda Britten, a writer and speaker whose specialty is dealing with fear. She says the voice of fear includes shame.

So if my inner voice says, "Hm, ministers typically make less money than reporters. I need a plan to handle that," it's actually the voice of freedom, of wisdom.

But if the voice says, "You're going to starve and everyone will know you were stupid to leave a perfectly good job. You always make the wrong choice!" then that's the false voice of fear. That's the destructive inner critic bringing shame.

Don't be surprised if the inner critic is shouting all day as you attempt to leave the hallway. Anything new is frightening. Change is anathema to this whimpering inner child, tugging you away from risk.

QUIETING THE INNER CRITIC

Amy Ahlers, a life coach and bestselling author of *Big Fat Lies Women Tell Themselves* and *Reform Your Inner Mean Girl,* bases her practice on helping others overcome that discouraging inner voice. She has created a tool called the Wake-Up Call Three Step Process that I've found useful.

1. Let the inner critic rant. You might even write down everything it says. Let it tell you what a fool you are and have always been. Let it tell you all the reasons that whatever you are contemplating won't work. If you're like me, you'll be shocked at the vitriolic diatribe that has been running in your head. You would never speak so abusively to another person nor let them speak to you that way. But you might have been disparaging yourself for years, and now that crazy voice is shouting at you on the threshold of new life, perhaps freezing you in place. Let it all surface, in order to be healed.

2. Then tune into the other voice within, your Higher Self or Inner Wisdom. Close your eyes, take a breath and ask, "What does my Inner Wisdom know?" Ask what it knows to be true about you. Listen carefully;

its voice is much quieter than the critic. Believe what you are told. You are love, you are beauty, you are safe, you are on track, all is well. Amy Ahlers says this is not forced optimism but a reminder of who you are and your soul's purpose.

The voice of Inner Wisdom can even be trusted to tell difficult truths. *Put down the cookie, sweetheart.* Or, *It's time to leave this relationship.* You are hearing the voice of Inner Wisdom when you feel loved, not berated.

3. Finally, anchor your inner wisdom with a physical gesture, such as tapping your wrist or chest. Later, the gesture alone can revive your feeling of serenity.

Nearly everyone I know has an inner voice that shrieks insults or, at the very least, cautions against change.

Mine has been highly active during the writing of this book, running incessantly like an annoying radio in the background. If you are reading this book now in any published form, you are witnessing the triumph of inner wisdom over fear. No matter how many years it took!

Again, I offer you recommendations from those who have been through the hallway before you. Here are methods of asking for help, human and divine:

* Be still, listen, sit with whatever comes to you
* Pray, meditate
* Open to your Higher Self
* Ask for awareness
* Ask for inner wisdom or truth
* Ask others for input and sit with their suggestions
* Ask to have blocks removed
* Answers will come from within you

* God and unseen helpers are on hand
* Practice the presence of love
* Move from head to heart
* Share experiences of the hallway
* Love your pets and let them love you

Incredible love is available to you now, as it has been throughout your hallway experience. Avail yourself of it.

BITS OF WISDOM

* What a joy it is for friends, family and spiritual groups to see you emerging from the hallway! Let them help.
* Critics may be agents of the Universe, helping you clarify what you want and why you want it.
* Your inner critic loves you and does not want you to fail. Just remember it is driven by fear.
* Check with your inner wisdom. What does it know? How can it set you free?
* Focus on the love and support you are receiving from others, and celebrate your own changes.

THIS PRAYER IS FOR YOU

As you get on with your life, remember that you have a staff of helpers eager to assist you. Some are friends or family that you can name. Others are angels or guides you might not see.

Call this energy God or Jesus or Buddha, in whatever form you imagine the divine shows up.

You are surrounded by the love of All That Is, which supports you in any endeavor. You have within yourself all the courage and steadfastness you need, drawing on the Source of life and love.

And you have human friends and family who will allow God to express through them to support you. Even their fears for you express their love.

The Universe is conspiring in your favor. Love is flowing to you from every direction, seen and unseen. Open yourself to receive.

22 Finally, Take Action

Now it's time to *do something.*

These ideas for working your way through the hallway and creating the next door probably won't be a linear process, and some parts might seem to happen all at once. You might be looking for a new job, for instance, while still struggling to forgive your old boss.

Just note that action is not the first step. Or the second or third. A great deal of work might go into shifting consciousness and creating conditions before action is likely to be successful.

By this point, however, any action will do. Any tidbit of activity will signal to you and the Universe that you are ready to move on. This might start with simple actions—catching up on chores or going to lunch with friends. You already have set an intention for how you want to feel; now pick an activity that might further that feeling.

One caution: This might not always be fun.

"DAMMIT, DON'T JUST SIT HERE"

The first year after Judith's husband died, she decided to go to a Fourth of July parade, a corny and homespun affair in her small town.

"I waited til the last minute and thought, Dammit, don't just sit here and feel sorry for yourself! Put a baseball cap and sunglasses on, so nobody will see how you look, and take off.

"I was, of course, feeling sorry for myself because nobody wanted to go to the parade with me. I guess I could have picked up the phone and asked somebody, but I didn't.

"So I'm walking down to the parade by myself, thinking, This really sucks. But I can't just sit home. The funny thing is, you're damned if you do and damned if you don't."

In town, she ran into friends, a long-married couple who were having a little spat. Nothing ugly, just a wife disagreeing with her husband.

"It waved over me—if she knew he was going to die a year from now, would she talk to him like that?"

For a long time, whenever Judith saw couples out in public, she would think: *One of you is going to die, and the other is going to hurt like hell.*

Taking action might not be fun at first, and it might not get your mind out of the hallway. Do it anyway. Get up, get dressed, go out in the sunlight and put one foot in front of the other.

This is the time to be practical. Send out resumes or get fertility treatments or audition for the play—whatever is yours to do. Make a list of actions that could move you toward your vision and research them. Let the Universe offer up variety. Try something new.

Remember, your consciousness already has shifted to start moving you out of the hallway. Keep looking ahead. Take small, positive steps every day.

FRANTIC ACTION

Just don't confuse action with healing. Some people in the hallway withdraw into the dark while others bury themselves in busyness.

Judith, the parade-goer, made that mistake just six weeks into widowhood. After nursing her husband through pancreatic cancer, she had hardly scattered his ashes when she decided to move her parents, both in their 90s, out of their distant city and into her home.

"I thought, This is gonna be great. I'm in a taking-care-of mode, and it will give me something to help someone else. I thought that was going to be a way for me to completely forget about how lonely and sad I was.

"It didn't work—it was worse. Instead of having a loving partner who was sick and needed me, they were two mean, ungrateful people ordering me around like a slave, criticizing me if I decided to go out with a girlfriend. It was miserable."

She moved them into assisted living. Her mother accused the staff of stealing, while her dad thought he was being poisoned. Judith assured the staff: "They're not getting older—they've always been this way!"

The facility quickly gave up on the pair, and her parents moved back to their own city.

"When they were gone, I was back in this void again," Judith said. "I went back to being a widow and feeling lonely again. It was like starting over at ground zero."

So she tried online dating. She had one dinner date.

"He could not have been nicer, but it was just, you know, we obviously didn't fit. He was quantum physics and all this higher math stuff. It was very left-brain. He was interesting to talk to. I could have sat and listened to him lecture all night, which he did."

Then halfway through dinner, he suddenly offered to fly her to Las Vegas and said, "I could fall in love with you."

"Why would somebody say that after knowing you for an hour?" Judith wondered. "Here's another desperate person!" Turned out his wife had died just months earlier.

This is why leaping into action is not the first step to take in the hallway. Or the second or third.

So how do you know when it's time to act? How can you be sure you're not rushing through the first door you see? Or forcing one open?

Back to the consciousness shift. Are you running from pain or moving toward a vision? You have already declared how you want to *feel*. Does whatever you want to *do* further those feelings? Are you running from where you are, or consciously moving toward something new?

Judith felt obligated to get on with her life, so she tried one thing after another before she was ready. In time, however, she reconnected with a man she had known in high school, who had been her date to the junior prom. When they finally married, their wedding invitations included a black and white snapshot showing the two of them as teenagers, all dressed up on prom night, 59 years earlier.

Girls are told they'll have to kiss a lot of frogs before they find their prince. You probably will have to open a few doors and at least look through them before you step across a threshold for good.

MAKING THE RIGHT MOVES

How exactly do you know when it's the right time to take action? You have shifted consciousness, you know what you desire for the future—or at least how you want to feel—and you have asked for help from God and humans. But what do you *do*?

I wish I could say "you'll just know," but you might not. You might make mistakes and have some false starts, as Judith did. That's okay.

It's unlikely you will come through a time of major change in your life and open a door directly into your ultimate destiny. The door might reveal only the first few steps on a path, then a few more, then a few more as you keep moving forward. We've all taken a few small steps that led to something greater.

You might also wonder when to hold onto your vision, waiting for just the right doorway to open, or be practical and take what's available. I'm not suggesting that you affirm your beautiful dream every day while you go broke, lose your house or skip meals. Sometimes you have to flip burgers to pay bills.

That's okay, too. The actions you take at this point in your hallway experience might be consciously temporary.

It is quite possible to take a temporary job—or, I suppose, be in a temporary relationship—without settling for less than you've envisioned. Settling is just that; you stop moving forward. You say, "This is enough."

But if you remain aware that your situation is temporary, you can be busy in one place while eager for more. Desire is the driver, remember? Your deepest longings will be your destiny. You don't have to sit home and wait.

So watch for opportunities. Remember they might be small. They might not look the way you expected. Pay close attention to inner nudges—your intuition is on your side.

Then take inspired action. Inspired action is not what you think you should do, but what you want to do. What excites you most? What intrigues you, pulling you to something new, even if it's completely unfamiliar? Is this the time to pursue creative arts or entrepreneurship or public service? What have you always thought you'd like to do someday? What did you set aside as a young adult, thinking it had no place in your grown-up life?

Show me my perfect place of service is a powerful, all-purpose prayer. It lets the Universe know you are available for more, no matter what else you are busy doing. Your place of service might be a paid job or not; might be with family, friends or new acquaintances, and might be a surprise or fulfill a long-held dream.

You get to design your life. What do you want behind the next door?

COURAGE TO FLY

Jack wanted to leave his lucrative job in marketing to pursue acting full time, but first he had to overcome some financial fears. He emailed me:

"In October, I started saying that when I returned after Christmas vacation, I was going to walk in and quit my nice-paying marketing job. Then, as I wanted to put more time into the acting career, I started saying that I would quit after Christmas . . . if not sooner! Then I started saying, 'Wouldn't it be great if I just got laid off and got some severance pay and extra time to prepare for January when the number of acting jobs starts increasing?'

"Can you guess what happened? Within two weeks, I walked into work and, after five years of being at that company, they had layoffs that included me. Wow! What a blessing! I got severance, vacation pay, plus health insurance benefits for a few months. Do I feel like I co-created this with God? Absolutely!"

But even with a small financial cushion, Jack was going to need work pretty soon. This is how he stayed calm and centered:

THE PAST: I would remind myself of the seemingly infinite synchronicities that led me to this point. I knew I was being pushed off the cliff to be taught how to fly.

THE PRESENT: I would stop and remind myself that I am a divine spiritual creation of God, and that God takes perfect care of me every day, in every way, always. No questions asked.

THE FUTURE: Once I had grounded myself back into the *now* and released worry or anxiety, I would then go back to making my co-creation affirmations for building the future.

Even while he was in the hallway, Jack said it wasn't hell. "It is a hallway filled with right opportunities and all of my dreams behind every door. And each door will be opened to me in the proper timing."

Jack added: "Enjoy the hallway while you are there. It can give you time to breathe."

BITS OF WISDOM

* Leaving the hallway is not linear. You might start taking action while still surrendering and forgiving.
* Taking action might not seem fun at first. Get dressed anyway. Your attitude is your choice.
* Are you running away from pain or moving toward a vision?
* You might look through a lot of doors before you step across a threshold.
* Being in the hallway might give you time to breathe.

THIS PRAYER IS FOR YOU

As you move into action, whether you feel tentative or eager, remember you are not alone. All the human and divine help you have drawn to you is supporting you now. Pause, be silent and feel the love surrounding you.

Let life unfold in its own time. You are working with a great and wise Power that gives only your best.

Pray: *Show me my perfect place of service.* Signal that you are ready to be and do more, and know that you are guided to right action now.

You might hear the latch on a new door being released.

23 Why Isn't It Working?

"I've done everything, and I'm still in the hallway!"

I hear this most often from people who expect their hallways to lead to some tangible change—a job, a new career, a baby, a relationship, even the sale of a house. But impatience sets in as well for those who are slogging through a long illness or grieving a permanent loss, those who only want to feel better.

Shouldn't this be over by now?

Pam is a lovely, smart, talented woman with expertise in database management, who lost her job and didn't find another one for 3 ½ years. She watched others come and go in the hallway, even celebrated with them as they left. But a door wouldn't open for her.

"It's day 1,296," Pam wrote me. "I work to stay optimistic. I wonder what's wrong with me and certainly know others wonder—*Why is she still in that hallway?* I feel like defective merchandise. I'm perplexed with what it is that continues to move me forward with hope instead of giving up."

With hope, Pam got dressed and drove to yet another job interview. This time, she received an offer.

"The RIGHT offer. After accepting, I sat in a meeting with about 300 people and was absolutely overcome with knowing—*This is where I belong.* This happened quickly and effortlessly. Anything which could have been a barrier simply rolled out of the way."

The moral of Pam's story? It takes as long as it takes.

I know you probably hate hearing that, and I'll give you further ideas for moving out of the hallway. But often it's not until later—sometimes years later—that you see why every minute you spent in transition was necessary. You were changing, and at the same time, people and events were moving into place for you.

Pam worked hard to understand the delay. "Maybe the hallway is a place of intervention. Maybe it is a way for us to stop so we can be reconfigured and guided on our path. Maybe it is the place we go to find ourselves.

"I have a perspective of what occurred in that hallway, but I also know I will look back over the years and see something deeper which I can't fathom at this moment."

ELEMENTS OF DESIRE

Following your bliss or finding your passion is sage advice, but it's easier said than done. A common delay in the hallway comes from not knowing what you want. If that's the case, you already know the answer: Figure out how you want to *feel.*

Remember your desires are communication from the divine within, prodding you to something greater.

Sometimes you might not be able to name a specific desire or passion; you just know you're restless. So make a list of how you want to *feel.*

* Useful
* Rewarded
* Energized
* Appreciated

You may choose from dozens of adjectives to describe the feelings you would like to bathe in every day. Apply them to work, relationships, health, money—any desires you can imagine. How do you want to feel in these areas?

Declare your intended feelings to the Universe, and watch what shows up.

Another way to home in on your passion is to list the elements of what you would prefer, as if you were sorting out pieces to be assembled in a puzzle.

Andrea was ready to work but had no idea what kind of job to look for. So she listed the elements of the job she wanted:

* Part-time
* Near her home
* In service to others
* Surrounded by friendly and interesting co-workers
* A chance to be outdoors

That's all it took. She happened to hear about a job at an addiction recovery center that she hadn't known existed, just three miles from her home. There, she was in service to others, working with friendly and interesting co-workers, and she was outdoors walking around campus all day.

You don't need a grand, detailed vision to start moving out of the hallway.

PERMISSION TO LEAVE

Even more common than not knowing what you want is thinking you do know, and knocking on the wrong doors. I'll always remember my friend Tim, who lost a job in corporate communications and worked for months trying to get an identical job.

One mistake he made was to attend networking meetings with other unemployed corporate communicators, all of them talking about how awful the job market was and how nobody was hiring. Tim would go home feeling hopeless.

But as he worked through the hallway, he stumbled upon a deeper truth. He didn't want to work in corporate communications again. Like Jack in the previous chapter, Tim had always wanted to be an actor.

All Tim had to do was acknowledge his deeper desire, and doors started flying open for him. He is still working as a professional actor and used his communication skills in marketing for a theater company.

So it's worth asking, Are you knocking on the right door? Do you really want what is behind it? Or are you attached to an outdated goal, something you once wanted but have outgrown, or something others want for you?

Delay in the hallway might give you a chance to release an old goal and identify a new passion.

Damon graduated from the Navy's Aviation Officer Candidate School in Pensacola and was assigned to Corpus Christi for flight training. But the Navy was short of instructors, and the students had to wait. For six months, Damon called in every day, only to be told he wouldn't be flying yet. He couldn't take leave because training might begin at any time. So he waited.

"Having that long a period with no work responsibilities may seem like heaven to some people, but for me it was a purgatory," Damon wrote. "Having a long time to think about life, I decided I did not want to be an aviator and that I was better suited for being a lawyer."

Even as his deeper desires became clear, Damon finally got his chance to fly jets. He earned his wings, then left the Navy. And stalled again. He was convinced his undergraduate grades would never get him into law school, so he got an MBA instead.

(Notice, even when Damon knew what he wanted, he assumed he couldn't have it. A common hallway mistake.)

Then one day he ran into an old friend who said, "Why aren't you in law school? You are one of the smartest guys I know."

"I told him that I could not get in. He said, 'You were a Navy pilot, we can get you in.'"

Today Damon is practicing law because flight training was delayed for six months, which at the time seemed a terrible waste.

"As you said, no door is ever closed without another opening for us," Damon wrote to me.

Tim and Damon gave themselves permission to leave their declared career paths to satisfy their deeper desires. At least a few people were shocked and worried by their choices. How could he give up a chance to fly jets? How many people make a living as an actor? What were these guys thinking?

To leave the hallway, you might have to risk others'

disapproval. You might be the one moving on while others linger. You might feel guilty or selfish.

So if it helps, give yourself conscious permission to leave the hallway. Try writing a permission slip for yourself. "I, _____, am hereby free to leave the hallway and walk through the next door." Your signature.

Maybe it's silly, but it's one more little shift in consciousness.

Or ask for permission. Ask the Universe, God, the angels, your Higher Self, the life force, your inner wisdom.

First, ask whether you have more to learn in the hallway or whether you are complete with it. Can you check this box and move on? You might be surprised at the clarity of the answer.

I remember longing for months to leave a particular job and feeling consistently guided—okay, ordered—to stay where I was. Until one day when I knew I was free to go. I remember the moment; I remember where I was standing. It was as if a bell rang, signaling the end of my need to stay in that job. I had permission to leave.

Be alert for messages of permission that say your hallway work is over and you are free to go.

FAILURE MAY BE NECESSARY

Every successful person has at least one story of spectacular failure. Seth Godin, an author, speaker and businessman, says his success is built on what he learned through failures. I heard Susan Sarandon say in an interview that her acting career developed because all her other plans failed.

The macho dictum that *failure is not an option* is ridiculous. Failure is always possible and might even be a necessary component of later success.

But oh, it's painful to go through. What if you try to follow your bliss, and your bliss doesn't seem to want you?

Carla is a petite blonde with a big voice. *Angel* is the word most often used to describe her singing. But somehow she can't manage to make music her career. She doesn't want to be a rock star; she still has children at home. Teaching music in the schools would be fine, or teaching private voice lessons, or performing in local theaters.

"Without exception, every door is closed up tight," she wrote to me. "I have always struggled mightily with self-esteem issues, and I take each rejection very hard."

Like so many people, Carla is trying to do everything right.

"I'm afraid my belief in spiritual principles has been challenged during this time. I've been to prosperity seminars, meditated for 15 years, visualized, tithed, volunteered and ministered, but in the area of my musical career and lack thereof, spiritual principle doesn't seem to bring results.

"I've spent lots of time working on my self-esteem, too. But it's hard to take one disappointing event after another and not make some kind of judgment about my ability.

"The only tool I have been able to consistently use is to recognize freeze-frame moments of good. Little moments—a kindness. a bird song, a smile, a joke. I have to make time to remember these moments, or I realize time will go by and I will have lost a big chunk of life being numb."

Even in her discouragement, Carla remembers to appreciate the present moment. She is not wasting time in the hallway, frustrating as it is.

If I were advising Carla, I might talk to her about divine timing. It's not that God withholds good until you're ready or believe you're worthy enough, although feeling unworthy is a big block to our good. Sometimes events and circumstances just have to line up.

Easy example: Let's say you have longed for a relationship, and at last you meet your soul mate. Why did it take so long? Maybe one or both of you was married in previous years. Maybe you needed to practice in other relationships first. If you had met sooner, you would not have been the people you are now.

Given that we live on a physical plane within time and space, the puzzle pieces might have to be arranged so your good shows up in the way you most desire. And that might take time.

WHAT BLOCKS YOUR GOOD?

Most of the time, delay in the hallway is the result of inner blocks, which could also be called psychological baggage. Your good is piled up on the other side of the door, just waiting for you to open it.

I've already suggested several beliefs that might keep the door shut:

* Not knowing what you want
* Not pursuing what you *really* want
* Not feeling you have permission to leave the hallway
* Not believing it's possible (Damon) or feeling unworthy (Carla)
* Or it's just not the right time. There's a bigger picture you cannot see.

But the simplest explanation for delay is fear. Old, familiar, mundane fear. Some of it conscious, some of it not.

The first fear is that nothing will ever change. You'll never get another job, never be loved again, never get well, never have money. Yet you're being admonished to think positively!

Mary was a single mother with seven children, two in college, when she was tossed out of work. She sent out more than 100 resumes, she interviewed, she networked, she worked temp jobs, she spent her savings.

"This hallway was dark and scary, and I lived in fear. I didn't know what I would do if I ran out of money. I was already doing everything I knew how to do. Selling a house would take time, and what could I rent with all those kids?

"I can't say I used spiritual principles. I just kept plugging away because I had to."

On the day she was supposed to start a second job, working nights and weekends to sell bedspreads at Penney's, she finally found a position in her professional field. It had been six dismal months.

Mary's enduring lesson was about fear. She developed

tremendous compassion for those who are unemployed and afraid.

"It is easy to say that someone should think positive thoughts and everything will be all right, that trusting in God will solve the problem, that it is necessary to believe in yourself and your future. My experience taught me how difficult it was to do that when I was the one in that situation.

"Yet I do think in retrospect that *I continued to attract unemployment while I lived in fear.* (italics added)

"I know now that everything worked for my highest good in the long run. But the long term is difficult to see when you are up to the eyeballs in bills, kids and lack of resources or prospects."

FACING YOUR FEAR

If the first big fear is that nothing will change, the second fear is that everything will change.

By definition, leaving the hallway signals change. Humans are hard-wired to fear change. Our most primitive brain warns us: *Don't leave the cave; monsters lurk out there.* Any change threatens our safety.

So of course you are afraid. Afraid to start a new job, to commit to a new relationship, to have a baby, to test your recovering body with renewed activity, to get back in the game in whatever way you've been out of it. You are venturing into the unknown.

Sometimes fear of change is greater than the fear of staying stuck. The pain of the hallway might be miserable, but it's familiar and easily mistaken for safety.

Then there's a lesser-known fear to face, one you might not expect. Joy. It's quite possible you are afraid of the joy that might be on the other side of the door. Because joy means change, too.

Consider this: Joy and success would be foreign to you now. You would have to become someone you are not at this moment. That would require an expansion of consciousness.

Remember consciousness shifts first. An inner change precedes anything new in your life. You might have loved high school, but you wouldn't have loved it when you were 6 years old. You weren't ready for it. First grade was all you could handle. Your consciousness has to expand, you have to learn and grow, before you can move on.

At this point in your life, you might require some inner adjustments and growth before you are ready to be joyful, before you are a match to joy in consciousness. Right now, joy might rank as just one more unknown quantity in your future.

So how can you overcome your fears, to keep them from blocking your good? Is there a way to hasten your exit from the hallway?

Think again about the paradox of creation and surrender.

* Are you clear on your desires, holding a vision of what you want, feeling the ways you want to feel?
* Have you focused on creating conditions through prayer, meditation or any of the ways you fertilize your spirituality?
* Have you surrendered, letting go of any outcome and trusting a Higher Power to work things out?

Which one have you leaned on most? Okay, then, start working with one of the others.

Again, a paradox is two seemingly contradictory statements that are both true. We create our experience *and* we surrender to life. We work with the mechanics of consciousness—visualization, affirmations—*and* we relax and know that all is well.

Through discernment and intuition, you know which to use at different times. But if you have been leaning heavily on a few tools, try incorporating different ones.

If you have visualized and affirmed and treasure mapped and written an elaborate vision statement illustrated with pictures, then try a simple prayer of surrender for the next few weeks.

Or if you have been relying on Spirit to take care of everything, try being more specific about your deepest desires. You don't have to describe a future that would be perfect for you. Just focus on the feelings you want. Joy? Peace? Confidence?

Go ahead and practice feeling joy, peace and confidence now, for no good reason. Then no matter how long you remain in the hallway, at least you will feel better while you're there. You will be lifting your consciousness with each passing day and, from that higher level, creating the life you want to live.

BITS OF WISDOM

✳ Working through grief, moving through change and creating a new life takes as long as it takes.

❋ Every minute in the hallway might be necessary to line up circumstances and prepare you for what's next.

❋ Are you knocking on the right doors? Check within to clarify your desires. They might have changed.

❋ Don't assume you can't have what you want. Give yourself permission to expand into joy.

❋ Every successful person has at least one story of failure. Failure might be necessary to later success.

❋ Freeze-frame moments of good. Practice feeling joy and peace for no good reason.

THIS PRAYER IS FOR YOU

You now have permission to leave the hallway.

Delays might give you time to clarify your goals and desires, even to change your mind about what you want behind the next door. A locked door or a detour might be moving you to your destiny.

You might fear the unknown. Even joy is unfamiliar territory, compared to where you are now. But you are being guided with every step.

Open your mind. Expect the unexpected. Notice people who are happy in jobs, relationships or cities they never imagined. Open your own imagination to accommodate your highest good, which is taking shape now to surprise and delight you.

This is a spiritual adventure, and you are perfectly equipped for it. You have everything you need.

24 Through the Door

Quick story: When I was packing to leave home as a college freshman, my mother followed me from room to room, trying to make sure she had instilled every moral value and bit of common sense she thought I might need.

Have I told you to lock your doors when you drive?

Do you know to study a little every day instead of waiting for the test?

Do you have an umbrella?

That's how I feel about ending this book and leaving you to your hallway experience. I want to make sure you have all the knowledge you need to move gracefully through change, even if life will never be the same again.

May I leave you with a few reminders?

Accept the hallway; don't resist it. This is happening *for* you, somehow. As soon as you can love your life the way it is and be grateful just to be alive, you will be moving out of the hallway. No matter how painful or unexpected, this experience eventually will yield gifts you could not have imagined or received in any other way.

Don't demand to see physical progress. You will *feel* better first; that's evidence of a shift in consciousness. You might sense your time in darkness is ending. But don't check every 15 minutes for an open door, like digging up a seed to see whether it has sprouted. Every time you ask, "Where is it?" you are focused on what's missing. Instead, keep your eye on where you are going. Having launched your desires, let the Universe find the best ways to mirror them to you.

Don't lose faith and don't settle. A temporary solution is not the same as settling. If you opt for a temporary solution, remember everything you really want is still available to you.

The Universe may be arranging the players and events to make dreams come true. Give it time. You'll be glad you waited.

Keep creating conditions for manifestation. Remember the spiritual work of the hallway is an inside job. You are being challenged to expand yourself and your awareness to meet the future. Ask for divine help and know you are loved and worthy of it all.

A MAZE OF HALLWAYS

You have probably realized by now that the door out of one hallway often leads to another hallway. Taking care of loved ones until they die is a hallway, then grieving the loss is another. Waiting to get pregnant is a hallway, being pregnant is another, adjusting to a new family member is another.

And some hallways can end only within you, when you learn to accept a permanent condition you might not have chosen consciously.

Kathy says her many hallways created a maze. After years of abuse, divorce, three bouts with breast cancer, remarriage, financial setbacks and a stalker, she wrote, "I am in the maze/hallway right now. I have been there a lot in my life. The difference today is that I do not separate out these times as *not* being a part of my life.

"I always used to look at these situations and think, 'Well, as soon as this is over and I get back to my normal life . . .' Wrong. These hallway experiences require me now to keep a perpetual 'hall pass' on the way to the next door that will open.

"Living in the hallway IS life. I believe there are moments of bliss and contentment and joy and arriving. But life dictates that I will pass through the hallway again. I'm just not as terrified of being there anymore."

Every person and every story is different. Hallways come and go and overlap. But the invitation of the hallway is for spiritual growth, deeper understanding and the expanded consciousness we sought when we came into human form. These are the experiences that make up a life.

MASS HALLWAYS

It has occurred to me in the writing of this book that we, as a society and as the human species, are in the hallway. Much that is familiar is dying or collapsing, doors are closing, and we don't know what the future will be. Even our survival on this planet is not guaranteed.

But as with any hallway, events that may be painful and messy at first—or even disastrous—can lead to a threshold we could not have crossed without leaving the old behind and wandering in darkness for a while. The old ways served us once but no longer function or fit our needs.

Some of the mass hallways I see, at least from my perspective as a middle-aged, middle-class American . . .

TERROR: I believe the attacks of September 11, 2001, put the United States into a hallway from which we have yet to emerge. It is filled with fear, blame and darkness, along with questioning and self-searching. We have declared enemies beyond our borders, and turned against each other within them. People in other countries are struggling to stay safe as well.

Where is the door to peace, and how do we open it? Are we moving toward a greater sense of oneness, realizing that war, starvation and despotism anywhere hurt all of us? Is anyone brave enough to stop the cycle of violence by refusing to retaliate?

PATRIARCHY: I believe we have opened a door to the rise of the feminine but have not yet crossed the threshold. What would society look like if masculine and feminine qualities were balanced? I'm not talking about a gender-based power struggle. Every human being is equipped with qualities considered masculine, such as achievement, competition and strength, as well as those considered feminine, such as nurturing, collaboration and intuition. Valuing all of these attributes might create a fairer world.

INSTITUTIONS: I believe we are in a hallway having recognized that many of our institutions—financial, religious, educational, political—serve only an elite and leave others damaged or disappointed. But where are the next doors? Could capitalism be made more fair? Is any organized system of connecting with God (aka religion) still viable? Is college worth the cost? Is democracy still the best option? This hallway of institutions is full of questions.

ILLNESS: I believe we are closing a door on a disease-oriented model of caring for our bodies and have opened a door to health. We are still in the process of releasing the old and creating the new. The healing hallway right now is a confusing bazaar of alternatives, modalities, diets and drugs. Once as I lay in a thumping MRI machine, I thought, someday this noisy monstrosity will be the size of an iPod. Then I thought, someday I'll be able to heal my body with my loving thoughts. Or maybe I could do that now.

Psychology is in a similar hallway, moving from *What's wrong with you* to a model based on strengths and positivity. It might include a stronger spiritual element, too. Talking to God—and hearing back—is not considered quite so crazy anymore.

DEATH: No matter how many people insist they believe in eternal life, most still treat death as an overwhelming loss and, in anyone younger than 75 or 80, a life unfairly cut short. Think how hard we work and how much money we spend trying to avoid death! The military-industrial complex and the medical-pharmaceutical industries are founded on our fear of death and efforts to avoid it.

Of course we miss and mourn those we love, and often wish we'd had more time before they died. But if we understood and truly believed they have only changed form, just as each of us eventually will, death might lose its sting. I see more and more people closing the door on death as a tragedy and opening to death as a physical transition that cannot end the life of the spirit.

I believe the burgeoning stories of near-death experiences and reports from the other side are guiding us through this hallway. I foresee an increasing number of people who will decide to skip the expensive and physically horrendous end-of-life treatments that might be available to them and slip away happily, knowing life has not ended.

I hope years from now, future generations might read this book and scoff at this list of worrisome hallways. They will say, "All those problems were solved so easily. Why couldn't they see it? Wow, things are better now than back then, aren't they?"

Of course that's the result we want from moving through any hallway and opening a new door. We hope to settle into a new way of living and, when we look back, wonder what all the fuss and fear were about. I hope all your hallways appear small in retrospect, with their opportunities and gifts now obvious.

PURE POSSIBLITY

What I love most about the hallway is its pure potential. Nothing has happened yet, and everything is possible.

You know the power of your of intention. You know you are the creator of your experience. You know the universe is biased in your favor. This is the beginning of the creative process, when the earth was without form and void.

"Don't be afraid to surrender to the void. The void isn't empty; it's filled with the divine," spiritual author Marianne Williamson wrote in a Tweet.

You are now in that moment of silence where you listen for the still, small voice of God. As you look at formless possibility, you set an intention and follow guidance to determine what shows up. You create your world as surely as God created this one, through thought and word.

It might not appear to be a perfect creation, but the work is never finished. You can't get it wrong because you never get it done. You are forever in the creative process in the hallway, moving through door after door.

The more consciously, the more deliberately and the more intentionally you cross the thresholds, the greater your spiritual experience as a human being, and the better you express and experience the divine within.

As a society, a group or as individuals, we may be catapulted into the hallway by sudden and tragic events we never imagined. Or we might be called into the hallway by our souls, eager to progress through their human endeavors.

The work is the same for each of us: acceptance, surrender, prayer, forgiveness, then taking responsibility to design our lives from this point forward, knowing all the help we need from heaven and earth is at our sides.

You are at the end of the hallway. Your life is waiting on the other side of the door. Open it and walk into the light.

BITS OF WISDOM

* ✳ Now that you have launched your desires, let the Universe find the best ways to mirror them to you.
* ✳ Remember the spiritual work of the hallway is an inside job. Life will change as you change.
* ✳ Hallways are a part of every human life. Sometimes one hallway leads to another.
* ✳ You might look back at this experience and wonder what the fuss was about.
* ✳ Welcome back to the light.

THIS PRAYER IS FOR YOU

At last you are emerging from a period of darkness in your life, never for a moment having been alone or abandoned, but always loved.

Now you know that you can accept these periods when you are in a hallway, let your experiences unfold over time, and affirm that your good is taking shape. Everything is part of a magnificent manifestation. This is all happening for you.

So as you pray for yourself or others, for our planet and our manmade civilization, affirm that the love and creative intelligence of the Universe is at work in each person and in our world.

We are moving, individually and together as human beings, toward peace, equality, health, courage and a world that works for all. Amen.

Acknowledgements

I am grateful . . .

To the many, many teachers and authors who have informed and influenced my spiritual growth, in particular Eric Butterworth, Mary Morrissey, Ed Townley and Abraham-Hicks.

To my friend Laura Shepard, who continues to be a guide on my spiritual journey.

To my mother, who first told me about the hallway, and who taught me to write.

To Janet Conner, for showing me the intersection of spirituality and creativity. JanetConner.com

To Samantha Bennett, for helping me over the hurdles of fear and procrastination and assuring me everyone faces them. TheOrganizedArtistCompany.com

To Nancy Barton, my book agent, who is also a meticulous line editor.

To Colin DeFord and Laura Harvey, friends who closely read an early draft and made invaluable suggestions.

To all those who listened as I honed these ideas in sermons, classes, workshops and conversations over the years, and who shared what worked for them.

To all who offered their stories for this book.

To all who encouraged me to write it.

Credits

Scripture quotations are from the New Revised Standard Version Bible, copyright © 1989 the Division of Christian Education of the National Council of the Churches of Christ in the United States of America. Used by permission. All rights reserved.

Amy Ahlers, "Wake-Up Call Three Step Process," used with permission of the author.

Ronna Detrick, M.Div., from her blog at *RonnaDetrick.com*, used with permission of the author.

Hafiz, from the Penguin publication *The Subject Tonight Is Love: 60 Wild and Sweet Poems of Hafiz.* Copyright © 1996 & 2003 Daniel Ladinsky and used with his permission.

Hafiz, from the Penguin publication, *I Heard God Laughing: Poems of Hope and Joy.* Copyright © 1996 & 2006 Daniel Ladinsky and used with his permission.

Hafiz, from the Penguin publication, *I Heard God Laughing: Poems of Hope and Joy.* Copyright ©

About the Author

Ellen Debenport is the author of *The Five Principles: A Guide to Practical Spirituality*, which is read and studied all over the world.

She speaks frequently at spiritual centers and conferences; leads classes, workshops and retreats, and has hosted nearly 200 shows for Unity Online Radio.

Ellen was a long-time journalist and political reporter who changed careers to become a minister and was ordained by Unity Worldwide Ministries. She served nearly a decade at Unity of Dallas, took a year off to write, then moved to Unity of Wimberley in a delightfully wacky town in the Texas Hill Country outside of Austin.

Visit her at *EllenDebenport.com* to subscribe to her blog, which reaches a growing international audience.

To the Reader

All the Bits of Wisdom at the end of each chapter are a suitable length for Twitter. I hope you will share them.

I would be happy and grateful if you care to leave an honest review of this book on *Amazon.com* or at *BarnesandNoble.com*.

And share the book with friends! Don't you know someone who is in the hallway?

—*Ellen Debenport*

CPSIA information can be obtained
at www.ICGtesting.com
Printed in the USA
LVOW10s1458170417
531099LV00011B/812/P